ASSIGNMENT Algiers

With the OSS in the Mediterranean Theater

Erasmus H. Kloman

NAVAL INSTITUTE PRESS
ANNAPOLIS, MARYLAND

Naval Institute Press
291 Wood Road
Annapolis, MD 21402

Unless noted otherwise, all photos are from the author's personal collection.

Library of Congress Cataloging-in-Publication Data
    Kloman, Erasmus H.
    Assignment Algiers : with the OSS in the Mediterranean theater / Erasmus
H. Kloman.
        p. cm.
    Includes bibliographical references.
    ISBN 1-59114-443-4 (alk. paper)
    1. Kloman, Erasmus H. 2. United States. Office of Strategic Services. 3.
World War, 1939–1945—Secret service—United States. 4. World War, 1939–
1945—Personal narratives, American. 5. World War, 1939–1945—Egypt—Cairo.
6. World War, 1939–1945—Algeria—Algiers. 7. World War, 1939–1945—Italy—
Caserta. I. Title.
    D810.S8K53 2005
    940.54'8673'0961—dc22

                                        2004028536

Printed in the United States of America on acid-free paper ∞
12 11 10 09 08 07 06 05   9 8 7 6 5 4 3 2
First printing

Interior design and composition: Alcorn Publication Design

Contents

Foreword

This is a memoir with a difference. While most memoirs are presented from the personal perspective of the author, Erasmus Kloman has gone beyond those confines to tap into the broader perspective of scholars and historians on the events covered in his treatise. Kloman's position in the three OSS posts where he served, Cairo, Algiers, and Caserta, offered him an exceptional opportunity to observe the workings of the operations sections of the fledgling OSS. But, as he points out in his preface, only after he began his research in the National Archives and his review of the literature on his subject did he achieve a more comprehensive view of the events in which he was involved. The hindsight gained with the passage of sixty years provides a basis for reexamining and reassessing those events, and throughout the narrative Kloman takes full advantage of new insights into the past, especially in his short epilogue.

Kloman was a young, newly minted artillery officer who, after OSS training in Washington, found himself thrust into positions calling for more experience and seniority than he had acquired. Having been reassigned from operations (missions behind enemy lines) to staff intelligence (mostly behind a desk), Kloman was in a good spot to observe close at hand the workings of the intelligence bureaucracy. His memoir throws a penetrating light on matters such as the competition and rivalry among branches of the OSS, the relations (sometimes smooth, sometimes anything but) between the American and British intelligence organizations, and the intricate political maneuvering of the Allied military commands with the emerging Italian Committee of National Liberation. His insider's observations on the controversial political situations in which OSS inevitably became involved are one of the chief contributions of this account. For example, the final two chapters discuss the issue of Allied support for Communist or pro-Communist elements within the partisan resistance and the related question of Communist sympathizers within the OSS.

Many of the subjects covered on these pages have been discussed in books and articles published in the intervening years. However, so much time has elapsed that the general public has forgotten much of the history, and Kloman's retelling may spark a new interest among readers, particularly among younger generations. Indeed, whether the reader is approaching this subject for the first time or after extensive prior reading, he or she will find an interesting account of the fast-moving chain of events, some seemingly quite improbable. The bibliography is a useful listing of the author's sources.

A bonus for the reader stems from the fact that Kloman presents numerous profiles of key figures, adding a dimension to the reporting of events. In the two chapters on Italy, for example, the reader learns a good deal about the personalities and motives of key players not only in the OSS regimental headquarters where Kloman worked but also in the several detachments to which he traveled on liaison missions. His OSS colleagues included an extraordinary mix, ranging from products of Ivy League institutions and the so-called establishment to the opposite end of the social spectrum. The wide range of clandestine operations that OSS carried out called for personnel drawn from all areas of society.

Kloman's experiences were not all confined to the business of the positions he held. He had more than his share of what he calls misadventures. For starters, the original mission for which he was sent abroad, namely to be dropped into Yugoslavia to work with the Tito partisans, never materialized for reasons presented in chapter 2. Kloman does not hide his lack of enthusiasm for parachuting, whether into Yugoslavia or anywhere else. Nor does he claim any credit for his advancement in the OSS regimental bureaucracy in Caserta, which he attributes solely to the good luck of being in the right place at the right time. Call it luck or chance, Kloman has taken advantage of his experiences to record the events he witnessed, the people with whom he worked, and the environment in which they operated.

The narrative presents a kaleidoscopic view of the military campaign in the Mediterranean and the political context in which it was waged, with glimpses of the Churchill, Roosevelt, and Stalin conferences and their influence on Allied military and OSS decision making. The invasion of North Africa is the first of the three major campaigns covered in this account, the other two being southern France and Italy. The OSS played increasingly important and valuable roles in each, learning from the book of experience, and this memoir presents an objective record of that experience. Kloman reports on both the failures as well as the successes of OSS operations, testifying to planners' need to take risks in the uncertain environments of wartime intelligence activity. The fog of war does not allow planners to count on certainty in any aspect. People and places change. Things go awry. In World War II, OSS was learning by doing, and the newly created organization's only mentor was its British counterpart, which often was none too keen to share its know-how with its American cousins. Kloman's observations on these sometimes rocky but mostly beneficial relationships are revealing.

In his effort to present an accurate and authentic account, Kloman has relied heavily on the literature of historians and scholars as well as interviews with the diminishing ranks of those who were personally involved. Their critiques of his drafts have added to the authenticity of the story.

Kloman faced a challenge in combining a serious record of the military campaigns and the OSS supporting role therein with a personal treatment of his daily life in the comparatively sheltered and comfortable surroundings of OSS regimental headquarters. His talent for artistry and rhythm have served him well in the effort to marry these dual themes. Kloman's war was nothing like the bloody experience of troops fighting on the battle lines or agents being dropped behind the lines. He acknowledges feelings of guilt about his easy life. This again was the luck of the draw, and he tells his story as it happened without spin or pretense. The result is a distinctive contribution to the literature, dealing with this important but relatively underreported part of OSS history.

John Waller
McLean, Virginia
May 2004

Preface

This memoir presents two stories wrapped together. One is about the Office of Strategic Services (OSS) and the important role it played in helping to win the war in the Mediterranean Theater. As such, it records the military and political events preceding and during my fifteen months in the theater. The second and more personal story, starting with my recruitment and training in the OSS camps around Washington, deals with my assignments in Cairo, Algiers, and Caserta. In these posts I worked with interesting people on interesting tasks and with a good dose of bizarre misadventures thrown in. Serving in the OSS was one of the most rewarding and, with a few exceptions, enjoyable experiences of my life. I owe a double debt to the OSS, first for recruiting me from the Field Artillery, the Army branch in which I was commissioned, and second for sending me to places that today are considered adventuresome and alluring travel destinations.

The good luck I enjoyed during the war stayed with me in conducting the research for this book. A huge volume of OSS documents had been declassified before I delved into the National Archives. On my first visit there I met Larry McDonald, the OSS specialist who had supervised the transfer and codification of these documents to the archives. Larry tutored me in the arcane ways of the National Archives and Records Administration (NARA) and helped me to locate documents critical to my search. Nearly every one of my requests for NARA staff to pull material from the vast array of stacks produced something of real value, and almost every new find led to other avenues to be investigated. My research turned out to be more of an adventure than a chore.

However, in the limited time (about four years) I could devote to research and writing, it was not possible to examine every archive file that might bear on my subject. As the endnotes reveal, this account relies heavily on authors who preceded me. By providing NARA reference numbers to key documents I used as sources, I hope to make this memoir a takeoff point for the interested reader's further research and writing.

My research during these years helped to restore fading memories of the events of nearly sixty years ago. It made me aware that the campaigns in southern France and Italy have received far less attention than the war on the Western front. In my view the Italian campaign, sometimes dubbed the Sideshow War or the Forgotten War, has received far too little attention considering the lessons it offers. Much can be learned about what went right and also what went wrong, both from a military viewpoint and in the highest political councils as Allied soldiers slogged their way up the Italian peninsula. The publication of Douglas Porch's major work, *The Path to Victory*, just as the writing of my book was winding down, filled a scholarly void and provided a long-overdue interpretation of the Mediterranean campaigns as pivotal in the Allied defeat of the Axis forces in Europe.

My research also made me aware of the relevance of the OSS experiences during World War II to current international conflict. The Special Forces, Green Berets, and Delta teams employed by today's armed forces can trace a direct lineage to the Operational Groups (OGs) and Special Operations (SO) teams that the OSS trained to infiltrate behind enemy lines. These were the two branches with which I worked most closely in Algiers, in support of the southern France invasion, and later in Italy. I was also in close contact with the Secret Intelligence (SI) branch that was first on the ground in the Sicilian invasion and prepared the way for the other OSS branches to carry out their diverse missions in the protracted and bloody Italian campaign.

Starting even before the Operation Torch landings in North Africa, the Mediterranean Theater served as a testing ground for many of the basic concepts underlying the OSS. Our personnel were learning on the job, while the military commands to which they reported were also learning what to expect and what not to expect from OSS operations. U.S. military commands today have come to a much fuller appreciation of the kind of intelligence and special-forces missions that the OSS offered.

In contrast with our closest allies, the British, who were old hands in intelligence and special operations, we Americans were neophytes having to play quick catch-up. A good deal of this story reports the ups and downs of our relationships with our British counterparts, which I observed on almost a daily basis. Among the transforming changes that have occurred in the six decades since World War II, one of the most remarkable is the role reversal vis-à-vis the United States and Great Britain. No longer the junior partner or latecomer, the United States is by every measure senior but heavily reliant on our British partners, most notably in the war in Iraq.

Reliving the events in which I was involved either directly or tangentially has been one of the principal rewards of this task. A major motive in taking on this project was to learn about the defining events of the campaigns in which I played a minor role. Originally, my intent was to write a private memoir for a limited audience of family and friends, as many of my contemporaries have done successfully. However, as my research and reading led me beyond my own experience into the history of the Allied military campaigns in the Mediterranean Theater and the OSS operations to support them, it occurred to me that my story could be of interest to a wider readership, including other veterans of the OSS and the broader intelligence community.

The idea of expanding a private memoir into a manuscript for publication began to take hold. Disregarding the old adage against switching horses in mid-stream, I plunged ahead with my more ambitious project, hoping to emerge safely astride on the far bank. When my publisher accepted my manuscript, it seemed that once again good luck had stayed with me.

Erasmus H. Kloman
Chestertown, Maryland

Acknowledgments

Many OSS colleagues and friends critiqued this memoir as it evolved through a lengthy succession of drafts. I am deeply indebted to them for their comments and encouragement. I have already mentioned the indispensable help offered by Larry McDonald, the specialist on OSS at the National Archives. His knowledge of the subject and his willingness to guide me to the most promising files made each of my visits worthwhile. Albert Materazzi, one of the original Italian OGs dedicated to preserving the record of their achievements, was an unsparing critic of my drafts and a source of numerous documents essential to my narrative. Two other OGs, both dropped behind the lines into France, Chandler Bates and Francis I. G. Coleman reviewed and commented on early drafts. Fig Coleman of the OG's Alice Team is featured in my narrative covering OG operations in southern France. William Woolverton, a fellow trainee in the Washington training camps and a roommate in Cairo, and Hendrik Van Oss, a roommate in Washington, both reviewed early chapters. Veva Wood, widow of Col. Martin Wood, under whom I served in Caserta, provided helpful background information. Laura Triest of the SI staff in Caserta read the manuscript and encouraged me to proceed with publication. Dan Pinck, OSS China hand and author of *Journey to Peking,* provided useful comments on one of the later drafts. Sarah Singer, a researcher at NARA, helped me greatly in retrieving documents and navigating the archives.

In both Algiers and Caserta I had the privilege of serving with Gen. Stewart L. McKenney, who reviewed several drafts of this story and provided valuable feedback. Emilio Q. Daddario, who worked in the top ranks of Secret Intelligence in Italy and with Allen Dulles in Switzerland to achieve an early surrender of the German and Fascist forces, critiqued the manuscript and offered the insights of a key player. After the war, Daddario served as a representative of his Connecticut district in the U.S. House of Representatives.

The late John Waller, chairman of the OSS Society Board, was uniquely qualified to offer advice as the memoir evolved to its broader concept, and I owe him a special debt. As a highly regarded author and an expert on the OSS, he steered me along a path that I have tried to follow to the best of my ability. The late Townsend Hoopes, a Marine Corps officer in World War II and former Under Secretary of the Air Force, proposed important changes in the structure and style of the text.

I am deeply indebted to my copy editor, Annie Rehill, for the finely tuned professional skills she brought to this project and for the great pleasure of working with her. My computer consultant, Chuck Engstrom, was an indispensable ally throughout the project, keeping me and the machine on friendly terms.

And my wife, Sue, a serious word person and literary critic, edited and reedited countless drafts, never showing signs that her patience was exhausted. To her I owe much more than I can ever repay.

Abbreviations and Acronyms

AAI	Allied Armies in Italy
AFHQ	Allied Forces Headquarters for operations in the western Mediterranean
Anvil	Initial codename for invasion of southern France, later Dragoon
ARSD	Air Resupply Detachment
CLNAI	Committee of National Liberation, northern Italy, abbreviated CLN. In Italian, *Comitato di Liberazione Nationale per l'Alta Italia*
COI	Coordinator of Intelligence, precursor of OSS
FANY	First Aid Nursing Yeomanry (British)
FFI	French Forces of the Interior
G-2	U.S. Army intelligence
G-3	U.S. Army operations
G-3	Experimental Detachment OSS unit attached to AFHQ
MEDTO	Mediterranean Theater of Operations
MI5	British domestic military intelligence service
MI6	British foreign military intelligence service
MO	Morale Operations, OSS psychological unit
MU	Maritime Unit, OSS maritime training unit
NARA	National Archives and Records Administration
OG	OSS Operational Groups
OSS	Office of Strategic Services
Overlord	Code name for Allied invasion of Normandy
RAF	Royal Air Force
R&A	Research and Analysis division, OSS
SFHQ	Special Forces Headquarters, London
SFU4	Forward arm in southern France of Special Projects Operations Center, Algiers
SI	Secret Intelligence branch OSS
SIM	*Servicio Italiano Militare* (Italian intelligence agency)
SIS	British Secret Intelligence Service
SO	Special Operations branch OSS
SOE	Special Operations Executive (British)
SPOC	Special Project Operations Center, Algiers
SS	Schutz Staffel, Nazi secret police
SSU	Strategic Services Unit, successor to OSS
Torch	Codename, invasion of North Africa
X2	Counter Intelligence division OSS
2677th	Regiment OSS Mediterranean Command (Company A: OG Operations; Company B: French Operations; Company C: Balkan Operations; Company D: Italian Operations)

1

Recruitment and Training
January 1943 to May 1944

*M*y class of 1943 at Princeton, which numbered 631 in our freshman year, suffered severe losses during World War II. Twenty-six lost their lives, and others sustained serious battlefield injuries. More than three-quarters of the class entered one of the military services. I was among the 60 percent opting to accelerate college studies in order to speed graduation from June to January of 1943. Fortunately for me, I had enrolled in the Reserve Officers' Training Corps (ROTC) program, one of the last mounted Field Artillery units. Although the horse-drawn caissons already seemed a bit anachronistic, it was a treat for those of us who loved horses. In short order I came to recognize that the chief benefit of ROTC training was that it saved me from the tough life and perils that enlisted personnel faced. As this memoir demonstrates, my war experience was, with few exceptions, comfortably cushioned and embarrassingly devoid of risk.

Because we had not received the full nine months of ROTC training during our final year, those of us who accelerated were required to go to Fort Sill officer candidate school (OCS) in Oklahoma. I am everlastingly grateful for the unseen hand that guided us to Fort Sill: in those three months, we crammed in much of the essential training we had missed at Princeton. I had been severely challenged just to pass through ROTC, barely squeaking through the dreaded written tests on the intricacies of the 105 mm and 155 mm howitzers we were trained to use. Equally daunting were the field tests where we had to actually fire them.

If I found the Princeton ROTC training a challenge, Fort Sill was akin to climbing Mount Everest. Fortunately, one of my bunkmates, another Princetonian named John Klopfer, took pity and tutored me to save me from the ignominy of flunking out. I was never comfortable using the protractor and slide rule to figure ranges and trajectories, but I did manage to pass all tests on the firing range as well as special courses in motor mechanics, signal communications, map reading, and so on.

Fort Sill's climate was as formidable as the instruction program. During our three months we encountered both bitter blasts straight from the North Pole and, later, torrid heat that we had to endure in winter uniforms, since summer

1

gear was not issued. Nevertheless, to my great relief and amazement, on 13 May 1943 I graduated from the Fort Sill OCS. The Field Artillery even judged me sufficiently qualified to win the gold bar, indicating the Field Artillery's desperate need for new officers.

My first Army assignment followed a ten-day leave in Baltimore with my father that sped by all too quickly. At my father's request I posed for a Bachrach portrait, presenting me in my hard-won second lieutenant's regalia. Along with a dozen or so other graduates from my OCS class, I was assigned to the Field Artillery Regimental Training Center at Fort Bragg in Fayetteville, North Carolina. Here our job was leading platoons of officer trainees who had finished various college ROTC programs. So we found ourselves teaching what we had only recently learned at Fort Sill.

After a few weeks at Bragg, the training cycle ended. Its graduates went on to OCS at Sill and were replaced by a new group of trainees. The new contingent consisted largely of graduates from Princeton and other Ivy League ROTC programs, and several men from the class behind me at college were assigned to my platoon. Many were better trained and more competent in Field Artillery weaponry than I, notably one soldier who had helped me prepare for an ROTC test. He and others knew how little I knew about the artillery business, which made for a pretty awkward relationship. Luckily my men seemed to understand the difficulty of my position, perhaps recognizing that we were all in this together.

On the whole, an officer's life in Fayetteville was quite agreeable—comfortable quarters, like those on any old Army post, and a good mess. There was a lively spirit of camaraderie, for we had undergone similar experiences and were all facing the prospect of overseas duty. The wives of several of the married men were quartered on the post, brightening life for the rest of us. I was especially privileged in that my father had given me an introduction to the family of a local doctor, a classmate of his at Chapel Hill. His two attractive daughters graciously included me and my friends in their social activities, thereby vastly enhancing my time in Fayetteville.

The training regiment at Bragg was one of many military installations around the country that the Office of Strategic Services (OSS) combed for personnel willing to volunteer for hazardous duty behind enemy lines. OSS Washington issued orders calling for an allotted number of officer volunteers to meet OSS manpower quotas. I assume that on this occasion, Fort Bragg was expected to provide three.

One day in November 1943, I was in the field with my platoon participating in a battalion firing exercise. A regimental command car drove up, and a staff sergeant emerged with orders for Lieutenant Kloman to report to headquarters. My first reaction was to wonder why I was being called on the carpet. Baffled, I

Portrait of the author

passed command to my sergeant, who was better equipped than I to direct the exercise anyway, and rode back to headquarters.

There I was turned over to another sergeant who had been assigned to interview me about "a highly confidential activity." I noticed that my file was on top of the sergeant's desk. I had to agree not to divulge the name of the organization for which the interview was being conducted. At the time I knew nothing about it, but the name and the aura of secrecy had definite appeal. Almost instantly I sensed that this might lead to my cherished desire, a way out of the Field Artillery.

The interview began with questions about education and pre-Army life. Had I graduated from college? Did I speak any foreign languages? Had I traveled abroad? Believing that it was in my interest to embroider the facts, I claimed a good command of French and extensive travel in France. In truth I had only the limited fluency developed in a few college courses, and had once spent about a week traveling with my parents in France. I reckoned correctly that the sergeant would not be able to quiz me on the language, nor could he learn how little time I'd actually spent abroad. The interview seemed to be going smoothly, and I began to relax.

Then came a much more frightening question: "Would you be willing to volunteer for hazardous duty behind enemy lines?" Possibly to be dropped in by parachute! Now the sergeant had my full attention, and I tried to conceal the turmoil in my mind. Remaining with the Field Artillery was not an acceptable option. Trying to seem in control, I asked some practical questions about training, such as where, when, and how it would be conducted, and especially what the jump training would entail. I can't remember how I phrased my final answer, but in the end I did volunteer.

With that the sergeant concluded the interview and passed me to another noncom, who commenced the paperwork to terminate my Fort Bragg assignment and transfer me to OSS headquarters in Washington as a trainee. I soon learned that two other officers from my battery, Bill Woolverton, the commanding officer, and another second lieutenant, John Birn, had also volunteered. In a short while, we three were on a train heading for the nation's capital. Serious about our pledge of secrecy, we said little about the interview process and the mystery organization we were joining, talking only about how happy we were to escape the Field Artillery.

John Birn, British by birth, had come to the United States partly to get away from his parents' unpleasant divorce, I later learned from his widow in London. He had worked at a series of menial jobs in New York before contacting the British consul, who'd pointed him toward the OSS. Calling promptly on that office, he learned that the organization was well disposed toward graduates of British public schools. The fact that John had graduated from Cheltenham stood in his favor. His interviewer told him the only impediment to his acceptance as a volunteer was his citizenship. But, they advised, they had the authority to grant instant American citizenship, and overnight John acquired his new status as an American.[1]

Bill Woolverton, a first lieutenant, class of '41 at Yale, came from a family well positioned in the New York social world. Handsome and tall, urbane and polished, he had no trouble attracting feminine admirers. Both John and Bill were to become my good friends in the months ahead. However, after our training John was transferred to the Far East, while Bill and I served together in three OSS posts in the Mediterranean.

Looking back on the Fort Bragg recruitment process, I am reminded of how lucky I was that the headquarters sergeant seeking to fill the OSS manpower allotment came across my name and called me in for the interview. Since I was in the first battery of the first battalion in the regiment, he did not have to search very far in the personnel records to find an officer with the right education and language requirements. Woolverton and Birn were also in my battery, so the sergeant would have found all the names he needed after a cursory search.

Another thought comes to mind about this recruitment process. In those days it was natural that a search for college-educated personnel speaking foreign languages would lead to the Ivy League and other Eastern establishment institutions. That was the biggest pool of personnel with these qualifications. For better or worse, they were part of an educated elite. Moreover, OSS was seeking not only operations personnel for hazardous duty but also the most highly qualified researchers and scholars who knew the languages, cultures, economics, and politics of areas around the globe that were of strategic interest to OSS. Before long the organization had brought into its fold many of the leading academics from top universities, especially Harvard, Yale, and Stanford, to staff its Research and Analysis (R&A) branch and other parts of the system needing such expertise.

Gen. William Donovan, founder of OSS, had attended Niagara College, a small Dominican institution with high academic standards but no Ivy League pretensions, for three years before transferring to Columbia University, where in 1907 he received his law degree. Franklin Delano Roosevelt was a classmate, and, although the two men belonged to different political parties, they became friends. During World War I, Donovan rose through the ranks to colonel and received the Medal of Honor, among other decorations, for his extraordinary acts of bravery. Idolized by his troops, who gave him the name Wild Bill, Donovan won national acclaim for his military record. He returned home to a hero's welcome, leading the elite 69th Infantry regiment in an exuberant New York City victory parade. Building on his reputation as a military leader, Donovan went on to develop a highly successful law practice. Though not born into the upper reaches of society, he cultivated those who were. As both a lawyer and a politician, he built a network of contacts in these circles. Thus it is not surprising that before long, word spread that the initials OSS really stood for "oh so social!" a sobriquet at least partially justified.

However, Donovan was by no means fixated solely on the upper crust for his recruits. He realized that for the kind of organization he had in mind, he would need a mix of socioeconomic backgrounds, including some with shady pasts. If a mission called for cracking a safe, a safecracker would have to be found, even if he was serving time. If the job at hand called for Mafia-type skills, recruiting from the Mafia was indicated. The unintended consequences of such recruitment, as chapter 4 on Italy will reveal, presented some difficult problems later on.

My two Field Artillery friends and I traveling to Washington knew little or nothing of Donovan or the OSS. Certainly we were unaware of being part of an elite. Our travel orders also included fifteen infantry officers who had completed parachute training at Fort Benning and Camps Mackall and McQuaide. In time, as we were thrown together in OSS camps, it became apparent that these fellows showed no visible taint of an Ivy League or Eastern establishment background.

On arrival in Washington, we three bewildered artillerymen reported to 2430 E Street, NW, where OSS headquarters was based in Que Building, located midway between a brewery and an old Navy hospital. After the initial signing in, we were assigned billets in something called Area F, to which we would be taken at once. We were hustled unceremoniously into the back of an Army personnel carrier, and the canvas hood was pulled over the back of the truck so that we had no sense of where we were going. We three squeezed in with the fifteen wild and woolly parachutists whom we were encountering for the first time. This was my introduction to the distinctive parachute troop uniform, pants tucked into high boots, regimental patches and wings insignia proudly displayed. It was also my first exposure to the macho ways of the parachutists, who yelled barracks-style expletives and shouted "Geronimo!" at each other.

Feeling totally like fish out of water, Woolverton, Birn, and I hunkered down and tried to become invisible. It dawned on me that these crazy parachutists actually liked to hurl themselves out the door of a plane, hoping that the parachute would open before they hit the ground. I began to wonder how I could ever have volunteered for this kind of duty. The further thought of "behind enemy lines" only added to my discomfort.

After a drive of about half an hour in the darkened truck, we came to a stop. An Army noncom, following an exchange with the driver, made a quick check of the passengers and passed us through. Since it was dark by then, we could make out nothing of our whereabouts other than the rows of tents where we were to be billeted. An uneasy night followed, in which sleep proved elusive.

Next morning after breakfast, we were given our first briefing. We learned that Area F would most likely be the first of five camps we would attend in OSS facilities around Washington. It was used for training personnel of all branches, especially the Operational Groups (OGs) and the Jedburghs, to which I was first assigned. The name Jedburgh came from Special Forces units trained in England, from the earliest days of the war, to work behind the lines with partisan resistance in Western Europe. The Jed teams parachuted in to resistance groups in France during the weeks following the Allied invasion of Normandy. A total of ninety-three three-man teams trained at Milton Hall in the English countryside.

Our three weeks at Area F were to consist of intensive physical conditioning along with what was described as "basic training" in close combat, demolitions, and the tricks of "silent killing" using the silenced .22 pistol pictured below. Our chief instructor was the legendary British major William Fairbairn, who had been assistant commissioner of the Shanghai Municipal Police for thirty-

Fairbairn knife and silenced pistol
Courtesy Congressional Country Club

three years. The Fairbairn knife was another one of the weapons used in our training. Happily I remember very little of this grueling regime other than how to furl a newspaper into a cone that, when thrust with force into the jugular of an opponent, can cause instant death.

In time we learned that Area F was actually the Congressional Country Club in Potomac, Maryland. The rows of tents we'd spotted on our arrival were located on what had been a vast array of tennis courts. Many in-the-know Washingtonians enjoyed joshing the OSS for training personnel in a country club. The program took us to four other camps in various places outside the city; between sessions we were responsible for finding our own lodgings.

After our first week at Area F, I asked my friend John Birn to come to Baltimore for a weekend with my father. On Sunday night, John and I, heeding the admonition not to reveal the identity or location of our training camp, told my father to drop us off in some deep woods a mile or so from the entrance to Area F. The next weekend, again in Baltimore with my father, I was astounded when he asked how I liked living at the Congressional Country Club. He was a serious golfer.

Area F was the basic or introductory course and an initial screening process to weed out personnel unsuited physically or psychologically for OSS missions overseas. A typical regime involved courses in four other camps at Areas A, B, C, and D in "secret" locations in Maryland and Virginia that the OSS had leased. By the time we were enrolled as trainees, a set curriculum had evolved, and each camp was designed to focus on particular skills that agents in the field required. I should note, however, that OSS was new to the intelligence game, and the training program was pretty much a work in progress. The agency borrowed heavily from the British, who had a few centuries of experience. We Americans were novices.

Major Fairbairn with his Danish assistant Hans Tofte
Courtesy Congressional Country Club

We were provided a nominal housing allowance between training periods. I struck up a friendship with a slightly older trainee, William Underwood, who had begun his law studies at Columbia. There he had been a classmate of Hendrik (Hank) van Oss, later to become a junior State Department officer. Bill and Hank were living in a rooming house downtown that had extra space. In those days it was almost impossible to find any kind of lodging in Washington, so Bill Woolverton and I moved in with them.

Firing range at Area F
Courtesy Congressional County Club

Underwood had a remarkable personal history, one that he kept to himself as much as possible. Later I learned that he had been born in Connecticut in 1912 of an American mother and a Hungarian father and given the name William Underwood Ignatius Posfay. The father was an irresponsible fortune seeker who deserted his wife and never contributed to Bill's support. At a young age his aunt adopted him and took him, along with his mother, to live abroad. They spent five years in Switzerland and later southern France. On returning to Connecticut, the sisters continued to provide a comfortable home for Bill. When he was ten he changed his name to that of his maternal grandfather, William Allen Underwood. He attended Kent School and Harvard, from which he graduated with honors in 1933. Having decided to study law, Bill went first to Columbia and then switched to the Yale Law School to finish his degree. By 1942 he was working in the well-known New York firm Sullivan and Cromwell.

Bill Underwood and I were together later, in Algiers and Caserta, where he became my deputy in the Special Operations branch. Our friendship continued long after the war, until his death in Paris a few years ago.

Our Washington lodging, which we dubbed the Grotto, had a colorful past. It was located in the basement of the Briar Inn, at 1527 Eye Street. At one point it had served as a "reputable" house of ill repute, before it was purchased in the mid-thirties by a Mrs. Johnson. She tried to upgrade the property by operating a cafeteria on the first floor and renting out the upper floors to "respectable young women." Later she also rented beds in the basement. The walls were constantly damp, if not actually dripping, thus the name.

Before Hank moved in, the basement at the Grotto had served as a Chinese laundry whose operator apparently had been careless about paying the rent.

Mrs. Johnson evicted him and installed five beds, for which she received fifty dollars a month each. Hank relied on ties with college classmates and connections in various government agencies to recruit a string of other contemporaries to share the space in the Grotto.

The OSS training program assigned particular roles to each of the camps around Washington. Depending on which branch trainees were assigned to, they attended a selection of camps to become qualified for their respective missions. The Jedburgh group with which I trained at first was being prepared to operate in three-man teams composed of American, British, or French officers along with a wireless operator. They would be infiltrated into France and other West European countries. Eventually, however, I was advised that my most likely mission would be in Yugoslavia. Although parachute training was obviously a vital part of the training, I was shipped abroad without it. Another big gap in my stateside training was the lack of both language instruction and orientation on the Yugoslav political and paramilitary situations. I suppose it was assumed I would pick this up once I went abroad.

Another camp I attended was Area B in the Catoctin Mountains of Maryland, later to become the presidential retreat Camp David. Here we concentrated on paramilitary training. My other camps have become a blurred memory. The bits that I do recall are like scattered pieces of a jigsaw puzzle. At several of them we had to assume cover names such as Student John. One camp gave us something like half a day of lock-picking instruction. That wasn't nearly adequate, of course, and in later life, when this skill might have come in handy, I had none of the lock-picking tools we had been provided.

Some time was spent learning how to steam open sealed envelopes leaving no trace of tampering. At Area B we had a couple of days of Morse code (nowhere near enough to function as radio operators). Considerable emphasis was placed on explosives, how to place fuses in various devices, where to place demolitions under bridges or on train tracks, and even how to attach limpets to the bottoms of ships. None of these abilities proved very useful in my later years.

The official history of the OSS explains the difficulty of training operatives in the skills they would need. Many of the circumstances for which agents were being prepared could not be duplicated in camps. For example, we could not fire our wide variety of weapons on live targets, only cardboard facsimiles. Also, the precise situation that any agent would face in the field could not be foreseen. Therefore a major goal was psychological: to train agents to respond rapidly and appropriately to unpredictable situations. During the final year and a half of the war, OSS assessment schools screened more than 5,300 candidates. Agent trainees represented about one-third of the 13,000 men and women who worked in the organization. The training was physically and psychologically rigorous; people were assessed for their ability to withstand pressures. Obstacle courses as tough as any in the military, lengthy night field exercises, and, often, graded tests at the end of a course sought to eliminate those who lacked the needed qualities.

One camp specialized in industrial sabotage. The OSS had made an arrangement with the Civil Defense Agency, through which OSS trainees were assigned, to develop covers for breaching the security of defense plants, thereby testing both OSS infiltration techniques and the adequacy of the civil defense systems. A team of several "agents" and a radio operator would be tasked to penetrate industrial facilities in one of several selected cities. In each city, the OSS had designated a senior representative to serve as a clandestine referee or troubleshooter. This person was informed about the project and instructed how to prevent the mission from being exposed. In Pittsburgh, the job fell to Edward Green, with whom I was to serve later in Caserta.

My team's mission was to penetrate the steel plants in Pittsburgh. First we had to work out our own cover stories, to be supported in preparing false ID documents such as draft cards, Social Security cards, and automobile licenses. The three other members of my team were Bill Underwood, Bill Woolverton, and Norman Randolph Turpin, a colorful native of Richmond who had completed paratrooper parachute training at Fort Benning.[2] As Underwood noted in his report, which I found in the National Archives, we had a three-part mission:

1. Penetrate one or more steel plants in the Pittsburgh area
2. Observe and report on production, assembly, and delivery techniques and on the attitude of labor toward management and the government; and
3. Plan a sabotage attack.[3]

Underwood took the name William Otis Greenough and adopted the cover of a reporter for *Harper's* magazine seeking interviews with senior union leaders and Carnegie–U.S. Steel executives. He was supposedly working on an article, "Steel at War," for the March issue. Woolverton's mission was to penetrate the same company posing as a job seeker.

My assignment was to penetrate the McKeesport plant of the National Pipe and Tube Company in Elwood City, just outside Pittsburgh. This company was working in three shifts around the clock to supply a wide range of gun barrels and other military ordnance. Heavily guarded walls and fences surrounded the plant. I had selected a cover as a college student needing a job to pay for next year's tuition. My cover name was Ernest Henry Klopfer. We were advised to keep our own initials so that we would be less likely, under pressure, to forget the cover. Also, Klopfer was the good friend who had helped me get through OCS. I rented a room in the cheapest boarding house in Elwood City and went to the employment office of National expecting that, with the tight labor situation, I would be hired instantly.

To my dismay, they told me that even workers at my low level had to go through a security check, usually lasting several months. This meant an abrupt end to my plan and forced me to consider penetrating my target surreptitiously, by a break-in. I had not contemplated such an exploit before embarking on this exercise.

We had been instructed to hold regular team meetings in different parts of town, so the four of us met on appointed nights in prearranged dives to discuss our progress. Our radio operator reported to OSS Washington on a set schedule. Bill Underwood (Greenough) advised us one night that he had succeeded in meeting members of the top echelon of United Steelworkers, including the president, Phillip Murray. At the executive office, a Mr. McClaine, head of public relations, had agreed to serve as his contact and to set up interviews with top management.

I reported that I was casing the security perimeters of National to find a place where I could break in under cover of darkness. I realized that I risked being shot by a guard or arrested if caught, but I felt I could not return to Washington empty-handed. In the waning hours of the last night before our mission ended, I scrambled through a slight gap in the chain-link fence and proceeded to walk around the plant. I spent quite a bit of time wandering around and looking for management's offices. Nobody paid the slightest attention to me, and eventually I was able to walk into what should have been a secure area, where I picked up a collection of documents and plant plans. Although in my haste I had no time to examine their contents, I learned later in Washington that they could have been extremely useful to the enemy and should have been kept under much tighter security. National Pipe and Tube would be ordered to jack up security.

I also discovered that I seemed to be the first trainee to actually break through security barriers into a civil defense facility, rather than relying on the assigned cover story to gain access. All others, until then, had successfully used their covers while incurring less risk during their stay inside the target facility. Bill Woolverton, for instance, had found no difficulty in obtaining a job as a metallurgist in his plant. No matter that he was totally unskilled, the need for trainees was so great that he was able to spend several days measuring the properties of metals at the Carnegie–U.S. Steel plant.

The senior officials who heard about my exploits regarded me as either a nut or a superhero, and for a brief while I enjoyed a certain acclaim. I recall an encounter in the corridor with Dick Helms, who was in charge of Special Operations in Germany and later became director of the CIA. He asked me—I assumed only kidding—whether I would like to take as my next mission a drop into Berlin. Not keen to find out if he might indeed be serious, I fumbled a response and made a quick retreat.

While I was enjoying my moment of triumph, I learned that Bill Underwood, aka the "Harper's *magazine labor reporter*," had run into trouble. Mr. McClaine, his contact, had called to ask him to come to his office immediately to discuss details of his assignment. It was apparent that the magazine had advised McClaine that there was no William Greenough on staff. After checking with the OSS referee, Edward Green, Bill had been told to cut short his mission and return to Washington. There he wrote a report covering not only his aborted mission but also the state of labor relations in the steel plants, as specified in our mission statement.

Our final debriefing was held in the Mayflower Hotel, where we were served numerous alcoholic beverages and encouraged to enjoy ourselves and drink up. Unknown to us, this session was part of our testing, designed to find out how well we could hold our liquor and how we would behave under its influence. Happily, we all had been accustomed to socializing with libations and were not challenged in this regard.

Before my last week of training, I went out to dinner with my cousin Tony Kloman and learned that he was in charge of all the OSS camps at Quantico, where I was to be sent. The OSS had four installations scattered around the heavily wooded five thousand acres of the Marine Corps facility. They were designated Areas A-2, -3, -4, and -5. I was sent to Area A-4, used primarily for basic Special Operations (SO) training. Tony also served as the head of training at A-4. That night at the restaurant, he took me aside to warn me that, since I would be using a student name at the camp, I must show no sign of knowing him. This seemed rather foolish, but I abided by his admonition and never let on that I was related to our camp director.

The obstacle course at A-4 was, in true Marine style, designed for the toughest and most combat-ready personnel. I remember keeping my head and the rest of my body down at snake level as we went through the exercise just as if live ammunition were being fired. What other tests of fortitude we had to endure have mercifully been erased from my memory, but I must have experienced a mix of emotions on completing the training course, a sense of accomplishment tempered by apprehension about the risks I would confront on my overseas mission.

What amazes me now, looking back on those days, is how little I was told about the mission I would be assigned in the Mediterranean Theater. My superiors informed me that when I arrived in Cairo and reported to the Yugoslav desk, all would become clear. Jump training would of course be provided as an essential part of my preparations, and I would be schooled in some of the military and political facts of Yugoslav life, about which I knew almost nothing. Beyond understanding that there were two factions of partisans, the Mihailovich and the Tito forces, I was pretty ignorant. Perhaps I was operating on the premise that the less I knew about what I was getting into, the less I would have to worry about.

Four and a half months elapsed between the time I was recruited and my departure for Egypt. Only part of that time was spent in the five training camps. In between we were on our own, and I do not remember any programs to inform us on how our training activities related to the course of the war in the Mediterranean. The curricula for the OSS camps seemed to be designed as generic training for would-be Special Forces, a little bit of this and a little bit of that in case it might come in handy someday.

Another gap in our training was any indoctrination on the overall organization of the OSS. As previously noted, the OSS had borrowed heavily from the British, in a sense our senior partners in the war. They had accumulated some five centuries of experience in overseas espionage. Their oldest organization, the Secret Intelligence Service (SIS) or MI6, began operating in the sixteenth century. An offshoot of SIS, Special Operations Executive (SOE), was created in 1940 to assist guerrilla movements in the war against Hitler, or, as Churchill proclaimed, "to set Europe ablaze." The British domestic military intelligence service was (and still is) MI5. Following the British lead, General Donovan and his senior advisers established a Secret Intelligence (SI) and an SO branch, each with its separate role. Essentially, SI was charged with espionage, the collection of intelligence, while SO was responsible for sabotage and liaison with underground movements. Soon it became apparent that these roles could not be separated in discrete compartments, but the organizational division was maintained throughout the war despite a good deal of confusion. Adding more complexity was Donovan's decision to create yet another branch, the Operational Groups, in which some SI and SO functions were merged. The OG teams were organized by target country and consisted of thirty-two men with some foreign language capability, trained to be dropped behind enemy lines in uniform.

Only after I had been shipped abroad and was finding my way around in Cairo did I begin to learn more about the organization I had joined. Even those in charge were learning on the job. Probably, if I had been more assertive, I could have found out much more about the overall structure and specifically what was in store for me. But I shipped abroad as did most soldiers, preparing for the worst and counting on superior officers of sound judgment. My fate was certainly out of my hands.

Because of the long delays in obtaining overseas transport, it was 1 April 1944 before I boarded a Liberty ship in Newport News, bound for Egypt. Bill Woolverton, Herman Nash, and I were the three OSS officers, and there were eight OSS enlisted men in our contingent. For some reason, Woolverton and I were assigned the task of running the ship's commissary. Twice a day we had to open shop to sell whatever stock had been put in our charge—toiletries, candy bars, cigarettes, nylon stockings, and two of the biggest sellers, snuff and chewing tobacco. We hoarded the unsold nylon stockings, dreaming of how they would be used in our romantic conquests once onshore. The commissary duty was not only a novel experience for us, but also a great relief from the monotony of shipboard life.

That boredom was interrupted, one night off the coast of Algiers, by a German bombing raid. Because our ship was loaded with high explosives, it was located in what mariners called the coffin corner, a slot on the outside starboard, or port, lane of the last row of the convoy. The theory was that if that ship were hit, minimal damage would be done to the rest of the convoy. However, in our case, the ship on our port beam and the one ahead of us both took serious hits and sank. We were hit, but the damage was confined to our steering system, and we began veering away from the rest of the convoy. It took quite a while to get an auxiliary steering system working. For several agonizing hours, our ship, instead of heading east toward Suez, headed west in lonely isolation, an easy target for another German bomber. Amazingly, none appeared. After a while, we succeeded in regaining control and eventually limped into Suez.

The last night on board, the ship's doctor gave a party for a small contingent of officers. He had saved up a supply of grain alcohol, which he mixed with grapefruit juice to make a lethal concoction. All I remember is waking up with a horrible headache, sprawled on the deck of the ship's bow. But, after a month at sea, we had reached our port of destination and the opening of the next chapter in our military careers.

A U.S. Coast Guard photograph of a Nazi bomber attack off the coast of North Africa appeared in the 12 May issue of the *New York Herald Tribune*. My father sent it to me soon after my arrival in Cairo.

Nazi bomber attack on U.S. convoy
Courtesy United States Coast Guard

2

Wartime Cairo
2 to 27 May 1944

*E*gypt was ostensibly a neutral country surrounded by nations either at war or on the verge of hostilities. Although it had achieved a qualified independence, it was as British as India under the Raj. Cairo's economy benefited from trade in high-end luxury goods while abject poverty prevailed in most of the country and neighboring states. Wartime Cairo was an extraordinary anomaly. A stronghold of Islam with numerous branches of the Muslim faith, Egypt harbored a mix of other religions as well, including one of the earliest Christian sects and a prosperous Jewish community. Over the years they had learned to live together, and there was virtually no discrimination based on religion. Nor was there any serious friction among the different nationalities represented in Cairo's population, which included, in addition to native Egyptians, sizable civilian communities originating in England, France (many traced their lineage to the Napoleonic conquest), Italy, Greece, Malta, and the Ottoman Empire, from the long era of Ottoman rule. It came to be accepted that Egypt, in those days, was a country run for and by foreigners.

When England declared war on Germany in 1939, Egypt broke relations with Berlin, established martial law throughout the country, and put all airfields and railways at Britain's disposal. The German population was rounded up and forced to leave. Though unwilling to declare war, Egypt maintained an informal, if somewhat equivocal, alliance with the British. On the news of Rommel's defeat at Alamein and the recapture of Tobruk, the handwriting on the wall became clear, and the Egyptian establishment began warming to the British and Allied forces. Although U.S. Air Force pilots had taken part in the air battle over Alamein, not until after the North African landings in November 1942 did U.S. soldiers come to Cairo in any significant numbers. In the beginning of 1943, American troops in Cairo, numbering about 1,000, were vastly outnumbered by the 126,000 British and Dominion forces serving under Middle East commander Gen. Sir Archibald Wavell. On the diplomatic front as well, the small American legation was dwarfed by the huge British embassy.[1]

British intelligence was represented by Special Operations Executive (SOE), created in 1940, as explained in chapter 1. It was functioning in high gear, with networks extending over wide areas of the Middle East and Africa. In sharp contrast, the United States was just beginning to build an intelligence capacity, and the first small base of the Coordinator of American Intelligence (COI), the predecessor of OSS, consisted of two officials who reached Cairo in April 1942. When my shipmates and I arrived two years later, the OSS office was still very small—a fraction of our British counterpart. For Americans like myself, who had seen little of the world and knew North Africa and the Middle East only through radio reports on the military campaigns, Cairo and all of Egypt seemed an extraordinary never-never land that we were entering without any idea of what to expect.

A headquarters vehicle met the OSS personnel disembarking from the Liberty ship in Suez and drove us the eighty or so miles to Cairo. My mind was in turmoil. Definitely on the plus side was the fact that we had weathered the Atlantic crossing, unlike many unfortunate souls on the two ships nearest us in the convoy. Moreover, I was excited to be in a country whose ancient history had captured my imagination since schoolboy days. But I had great concern about my mission into Yugoslavia. I had been given no practical information about such questions as where and when I would receive parachute training, the partisan group I would be dropped into, and the prospects for briefings on the political and military situation in partisan-held areas. I mulled these issues over uneasily as our vehicle lumbered over the road to Cairo. When it finally came to a stop, we were ushered into a building guarded by U.S. soldiers.

Along with the other new arrivals, I was led to the duty officer, who asked to see my orders instructing me to report to the Yugoslav desk. It came as quite a shock when the officer said that desk had moved to Algiers some time ago. Apparently he had not been informed of my pending arrival and had no clue about what to do with a stray second lieutenant arriving from Washington. It seemed that I had been entirely forgotten during my extended Atlantic crossing.

I told the duty officer that I would move on to Algiers to catch up with the Yugoslav desk. But instead of concurring with that proposition, he asked me to wait outside his office while he made some inquiries. When he called me back in, he advised me that I would remain in Cairo, at least for the near term. He had arranged a billet for Bill Woolverton; Peter Skurla, a U.S. Navy lieutenant; and me in Jan Smuts House. There, a house-man named Brassier would take care of the flat and prepare our meals. During our stay, we would continue the training for Special Operations with practice in firing captured enemy weapons in the desert. We were expected to report to headquarters every few days, to collect our mail and await further orders. To our delight and amazement, the duty officer also handed us guest privilege cards for the Gezira Sporting Club and the Royal Riding Academy, saying that we could use these facilities whenever we had free time.

Life seemed to have taken a sharp turn for the better, but before concluding his interview with me, the duty officer handed me a real stunner. While I was

Bill Woolverton, Peter Skurla, and me at our Cairo flat

in Cairo, he said, I would be expected to develop a Special Operations mission for myself. Never mind that I was a twenty-two-year-old, newly minted Army officer totally inexperienced in combat, with only the most superficial knowledge of the military situation in the Mediterranean Theater. Somehow I would have to devise a practical plan for the kind of operation I had volunteered to carry out when the OSS had first recruited me.

The reasoning behind this assignment still remains a mystery to me. It seems unlikely that anyone in authority could have seriously believed me capable of concocting a truly viable operation. Perhaps it was intended to prevent me from forgetting why I had been shipped abroad, to ensure that I didn't succumb to the good life in Cairo. In any event, I took the assignment seriously enough. After meeting a fellow from New York named Tom Stix, who was organizing a mission into Greece, I began working on a plan to accompany him.

Tom's mission called for entering Greece by sea in a caïque, the traditional Eastern Mediterranean one-masted sailing vessel. The objective of his operation was to radio reports of enemy ship movements from a high mountain lookout near the coast. My sole rationale for trying to participate in this mission was based on the fact that I had studied ancient Greek in high school and during my first year at Princeton. Since the old language bears only a distant relationship to modern Greek, I signed up for language lessons with an elderly Greek teacher.

Our training exercises with captured enemy weapons took place in a desert area some distance from Cairo. There we learned how to fire a variety of German

Firing practice in the desert

and Italian arms, including handguns, machine guns, mortars, and other weapons. We also received more training in hand-to-hand combat, similar to that in the camps around Washington. But since I had not been told what my mission would be, this training lacked the focus essential for a productive course of precombat preparations. We received no concrete order-of-battle briefings, nor were we briefed on the various fronts where the OSS was engaged or the overall military situation in the Mediterranean. We had a sense of going through paces without specific goals. No one in authority had reviewed my idea of a mission into Greece with Tom Stix.

Yugoslav partisans in Cairo (I am in back row)

Pete Skurla was working with a group of Yugoslav partisans who had re-mained in Cairo while preparing for their drop into their home country. I went along with them on a sightseeing visit, but otherwise I was not involved with that team, and I can't explain my presence in the last row of this photo.

When not engaged in the sporadic training exercises in the desert or study-ing Greek, I devoted most of my time to enjoying life. Compared with the bleak prospect of a parachute drop into the rough terrain of partisan-occupied Yugo-slavia, the goal of penetrating Greece via caïque seemed less daunting.

Wartime Cairo was steeped in the exotic aura of the waning colonial era. Reminders of British imperial rule were ever-present in the flags atop the British embassy and the barracks housing British and Dominion troops, as well as in such bastions as the old Shepheards Hotel and, out by the pyramids, Mena House. Every day saw numerous displays of the military might of imperial forces that had driven the Germans and Italians from North Africa. Most often the troops marched in battle dress, but on ceremonial occasions they paraded in striking regimental uniforms.[2]

For the Anglophile I was then, such outward signs of British influence were glamorous and reassuring. I learned only much later that upper levels of the British establishment barely tolerated the presence of American military forces in Egypt. Even less welcome were representatives of an American intelligence agency. Neither the British nor the French, who retained a lingering interest from the days when they had ruled Egypt, wanted American intelligence operatives encroaching on their territory. They were old hands, while we were untrained and, for the most part, lacking in the depth of knowledge of the region that our Allies had gained over the years.

British resentment of the Americans was fueled partly by our higher pay scales and living allowances. American enlisted men and officers could afford to pay far more for housing and other amenities than could their British counterparts. On the other hand, many Americans came to suspect that they were fighting a war mainly to preserve the privileged way of life of the upper ranks of British colonials. American GIs scoffed at the restrictions keeping many hotels and restaurants off limits to what the British called "other ranks." In many situations, British reserve—some would say stuffiness—clashed with the casual, more democratic outlook of the Americans.

Although the OSS had relied heavily on British intelligence techniques as a model in setting up its organization and the British were keen to have American military forces supporting their war effort, the British intelligence hierarchy was reluctant to accept the OSS as a full partner. Thus, in Cairo there was a fair amount of rivalry and bureaucratic squabbling between the OSS and the SOE.

However, at the level where my roommates and I operated, we were unaware of these rivalries. Before long we had made friends with a few British officers, and through them we also met some of the female volunteer equivalents of the U.S. WACs, the FANYs, members of the First Aid Nursing Yeomanry. We entertained a few of them in our Smuts House flat. The Brits, like their compatriots in colonial outposts all over the globe, knew how to lead the good life and were unashamed to declare, "It's a helluva war, but it's better than no war at all."

Clubs were an essential mainstay of British colonial life, and the Gezira Sporting Club was one of the oldest of these institutions, boasting facilities for all traditional British sports. Cricket matches were scheduled regularly, and a great many tennis courts were maintained. Dressed in their mandatory whites, members kept the courts busy except during the hot midday hours. Egyptian ball boys were considered an essential perk, and I managed to accommodate to this practice. I also took advantage of other club amenities, including the bars and lounges overlooking the courts. The staple concoction was gin and quinine, the latter said to combat malaria. Of course, all Allied forces, including ours, were issued quinine tablets as a more reliable means of avoiding that malady.

A common and unwelcome affliction among new American arrivals was "gyppy tummy," the Egyptian version of the common scourge in the underdeveloped world. Although we were warned against eating raw fruits and vegetables and drinking tap water, it was almost impossible to avoid an occasional slipup, and I succumbed more than once. I still retain a vivid olfactory memory

Lillé with admirers

of the urban squalor of city streets, traversed daily by lines of donkeys and camels making their contribution to the smell of untreated sewage, which in turn competed with the aroma of Middle Eastern spices.

At first, Woolverton, Skurla, and I took our meals mostly in our flat, where Brassier (whom we naturally called Brazzeer) cooked all the ingredients he had ordered from local markets. Since none of us had the slightest idea of how to run a household, and since Brassier was responsible not to us but to the Cairo OSS office, he was, in effect, his own boss. Before long we noticed that when we had finished dinner, quite a number of Brassier's relatives and friends gathered on the

A FANY and her friend

rear balcony. Brassier evidently bought enough food to serve this group as well. We assumed this was how it had been for our predecessors in the flat, and how it would be after we had gone.

Soon we were venturing out to the many restaurants and nightclubs flourishing in and around Cairo. While the famous Groppi's café, catering to a select clientele of cultivated European tastes, served fabulous pastries, ice cream, and strong aromatic coffees, a great variety of other culinary traditions were represented in the city. Fear of gyppy tummy and a concern for security usually caused me to avoid the local Arab places, but on a couple of occasions we did go to the Auberge des Pyramides, the best-known Arab establishment and a favorite of King Farouk, who was often seen there with one of his mistresses. We three very junior Americans were at far too low a level even to be aware of the scandals of the court, but Cairene society was abuzz about the marital troubles of the king, and about Queen Farida's contempt for his philandering.

Located in great tents on the road to the pyramids, the Auberge drew Cairo's polyglot café society to its gambling tables and bars. Representatives of the Allied military establishment mingled with the establishment of Cairo and its demimonde. Well-endowed belly dancers performed to the spellbinding music of

Arabian instruments. The setting was reminiscent of a Hollywood film featuring Peter Lorre, Sidney Greenstreet, or Marlene Dietrich.

A high point of my brief stay in Cairo was a visit to the archaeological excavation that Harvard was carrying out near the pyramids. One of the OSS enlisted men had come to know the woman in charge of the site. During the war, excavation was suspended; the dig was closed to the public, and the curator served mainly as a custodian to ensure security. But on Sundays, she would invite a few interested people for tea under her tent, which covered the site. When I expressed interest in seeing the dig, the corporal arranged for me to go with him.

My memory of the visit is sketchy. I recall that the curator lit the way with a flashlight, down through a series of dark passageways into various spaces where she pointed out the main features. Even though I was too uninformed to absorb it all, I realized that this was an exceptional opportunity to witness firsthand an important archaeological find. The visit initiated a lifelong interest in the ancient history of Egypt, and in the still-unresolved mysteries of its monuments.

Conversation over tea with the lady curator after the tour spurred my interest further, and I was invited to come for a return visit. But this was not to be. My stay in Cairo was about to come to an abrupt end.

Having begun to really enjoy life in Egypt while focusing on the possibility of going into Greece via caïque, I was summoned to a meeting with a representative from OSS Washington who was inspecting the work of field stations in the Middle East. I sat across a table from him while he quizzed me about what I was doing. I explained how my original assignment to be dropped into Yugoslavia had been aborted. Then I described the mission I had devised, involving teaming up with Tom Stix and learning modern Greek. I sensed, as I talked, that the headquarters representative was not impressed.

Evidently it had already been decided somewhere up the line that I should be transferred to Algiers, but not to be reconnected with the Yugoslav operations. Instead, I was to work with the group supporting OSS teams involved in the invasion of southern France. They were training to be dropped into Maquis-controlled areas, to assist in cutting off supply lines and sabotaging enemy forces there.

The Washington interviewer then surprised me by adding that I would be switched from an operations role to a staff intelligence role. The operations teams for southern France had already been formed and trained for their specific missions. What Algiers needed now was staff support: planning the specifics of each mission, maintaining radio communications with the Maquis (French resistance forces named for the scrub-bush terrain they inhabited), coordinating U.S. operations with our French and British counterparts, and briefing the teams on local situations in their drop zone before departure. I was being assigned as an intelligence officer to SPOC, the Special Projects Operations Center, a British-

French-American staff responsible for supporting all planning and overseeing Special Forces operations behind enemy lines in France.

My reaction to this switch was mixed. On one hand I was relieved that parachuting and the training for it were no longer in my future. But I also felt let down—deprived of the opportunity to meet the challenge. Not only was I being removed from the type of mission for which I had been trained, but I was also being yanked away from the mission into Greece. Many years later, I learned that Tom Stix successfully carried out that assignment. After landing his caïque on the coast, he managed to establish his base on the mountain from which he radioed reports on enemy ship movements, making the Adriatic waters safer for Allied vessels.[3]

I was sad to be leaving Cairo, which had exerted its charm on me despite its squalor. But I looked forward to seeing another legendary city, and to exchanging the British colonial atmosphere for that of the French. In any event, the decisions on what I was to do and where I was to go were out of my hands. I realized that I was only a small cog in the big military machine dedicated to winning a war.

3

Algiers
27 May to 22 September 1944

eparting from Cairo and arriving in Algiers meant adjusting to a new cultural environment. Wartime Cairo's atmosphere was quintessentially British empire; Algiers's was decidedly French. Instead of the Union Jack, the *bleu, blanc, et rouge* of the French tricolor and the occasional Croix de Lorraine flew in all public places. Streets bore prominent French names, and, except in places such as the mysterious casbah, French was the *lingua franca.*

The war had different impacts on Algeria and Egypt. Algeria was liberated from its status as a department of Vichy France to become part of Free France, while Egypt retained its neutrality. American troops played a pivotal role in driving the Axis forces from Morocco and Algeria, but in the eastern Mediterranean campaigns they played less of a role.

In October 1942, Gen. Mark Clark secretly landed on a beach about seventy-five miles from Algiers. His mission was to meet with anti–Vichy French military officers to prepare for Operation Torch, the codename for the North African invasion scheduled for the first week in November. Afterward, the United States became increasingly engaged in intelligence operations to ensure the success of that invasion. Roosevelt had designated Robert D. Murphy as his personal representative in North Africa, overseeing one of the intelligence rings run out of FDR's White House. It consisted of a cadre of twelve so-called vice consuls placed in strategic North African locales. Ostensibly, their mission was to ensure that American shipments of food and scarce commodities were not diverted to Germany or Italy. In fact, they were collecting valuable political and military intelligence. They submitted information vital to the landing operations, including detailed reports on harbors and beaches. At the same time they monitored German, French, and Italian military personnel in Casablanca and Algiers. The Vichy officers who met with General Clark, as well as others believed to be disloyal to the Wehrmacht, were persuaded to switch sides once the invasion was launched.[1]

Planning for the North Africa campaign gave Col. William Donovan, a confidant of President Roosevelt since law school, an opportunity to demonstrate the worth of a civilian intelligence agency. FDR enjoyed playing the role of spymaster and, despite strong opposition from the U.S. military establishment, encouraged Donovan to lay the groundwork for such an agency. On 14 July 1942, he signed the executive order establishing the COI, the Coordinator of Intelligence.

The concept of a North African assault was considered a dubious enterprise in U.S. military circles. Churchill sold the idea to Roosevelt as the one sure way to get American troops into action against Hitler. But Roosevelt had to counter the unanimous opposition of his Joint Chiefs of Staff, who saw no advantage in committing forces in the direction of Beirut rather than toward the main target of Berlin. Roosevelt gave his bold order despite the fact that at the time, the United States did not have a single fully trained and equipped division to contribute to this assault. In so doing, the president displayed his characteristic confidence in his own judgment as commander-in-chief, as well as the remarkable capacity to select or even disregard advice from others with whom he disagreed.

On 14 January 1943, Roosevelt and Churchill met in Casablanca for one of the major summit conferences of the war. This meeting may be best known for having adopted the policy of unconditional surrender as the iron law under which the Allies would engage the enemy. In addition to strategic and military concerns, Roosevelt and Churchill had to deal with the thorny problem of rivalry for leadership of the French resistance between General Charles de Gaulle in London and General Henri Giraud in North Africa. Giraud was struggling to put together a broadly based paramilitary organization under his command. Although de Gaulle flew to Casablanca from London for a brief reconciliation meeting with Giraud, their handshake before photographers amounted to no more than a façade. De Gaulle's prickly, prima donna personality was already much in evidence. Not until the last months of 1943 was he successful in outmaneuvering Giraud and forming an ostensibly united French Committee of National Liberation.

The power struggle at top levels of the French military posed a difficult choice for OSS leadership in North Africa. At first, OSS Washington favored supporting the Giraudist forces. However, liberal opinion, including some elements within the OSS, leaned toward de Gaulle. Indeed, a pro-Gaullist "cell" formed in Algiers among some of the academics in the small Research and Analysis branch. Led by H. Stuart Hughes, grandson of Charles Evans Hughes, this group believed that de Gaulle would ultimately prevail in the French political arena. Partly influenced by this assessment, OSS strategy shifted to support of the Gaullists.

Donovan had chosen Marine colonel William Eddy as his principal representative in North Africa. A casting director would have been hard pressed to find a more perfect candidate. Born in Syria of missionary parents, Eddy had been highly decorated for his World War I service in Army intelligence. He had taught

English at the American University in Cairo, and in 1941, when he reenlisted, he returned to Cairo as naval attaché. Walking with a slight limp from old battle wounds and wearing five rows of medals on his Marine uniform, Eddy prompted General Patton to deliver one of his wisecracks: "The sonofabitch's been shot at enough, hasn't he?"[2]

Initially operating from a base in Tangiers, Eddy worked closely with Robert Murphy in planning the North Africa invasion. Ironically, the invading troops would be fighting to regain territory controlled mainly by French forces, with only a few German units involved. Allied intelligence underestimated the initial resistance that would be encountered after landing, and the operation's many shortcomings cost the lives of nearly two thousand American and British soldiers. After a few days, however, resistance collapsed, in part because the defenders had been taken totally by surprise. Moreover, the majority of French forces had no will to fight and actually welcomed liberation from Nazi rule. An armistice was signed in November 1942. Allied Forces Headquarters (AFHQ) moved from Tangiers to Algiers, as did the OSS organization.

Colonel Eddy was given command of OSS Algiers, as an arm of G-3 AFHQ, with the designation of Experimental Detachment G-3. In the following months, after several name changes, it became 2677th Regiment, Office of Strategic Services. Four companies, A, B, C, and D, were established as subheadquarters, and their designations changed as the military situation evolved. The organizational structure was always in a state of flux, and fitting a quasi-civilian agency into a military command posed a nomenclature challenge.

OSS Algiers was located in and around Villa Magnol, high on a hill overlooking the city and its port. This sprawling complex housed all OSS branches: Special Operations (SO), Operational Groups (OGs), Secret Intelligence (SI), Morale Operations (MO), Counter Intelligence (X2), and Research and Analysis (R&A).

In its support of Allied Forces Headquarters, OSS Algiers was responsible for assisting in all facets of the campaign to defeat the Axis. Thus, the various branches housed in Villa Magnol were engaged in a wide range of activities on various fronts of the war, including southern France, Yugoslavia, the Balkans, Greece, Austria, and Italy.

In March 1944, General de Gaulle announced the formation of Forces Françaises de l'Intérieur (FFI), designed to unite the various Maquis factions of Gaullist, Giraudist, and Communist persuasion with the French Armée Secrète, the merged paramilitary reserves of the major resistance groups. But the FFI, in spite of de Gaulle's official endorsement, was more of an aspiration than a reality, for the several factions were unwilling to suppress their political differences. Nevertheless, the FFI played a very important liaison role with American and British teams by supporting resistance in the field.[3]

OSS headquarters in Algiers, Villa Magnol

Among the many projects that Donovan was eager to launch in his new organization, he assigned a high priority to the OGs and gained approval of the concept by the Joint Chiefs of Staff. The idea was to tap the cultural diversity of the American public, recruit volunteers who spoke foreign languages, and train them to conduct guerilla operations behind enemy lines. He named Russell Livermore, a prominent New York Republican attorney, as head of the branch. Since the OG training program was starting from scratch and had few instructors trained in this type of warfare, the early programs borrowed heavily from lessons learned by the British, especially Special Operations Executive (SOE).

The first four officers from the Engineer School in Fort Belvoir, Virginia, began training in April 1943, followed by infantry officer recruits and a contingent from the 100th Division. After attending Area F, at the Congressional Country Club, and Fort Benning for preliminary parachute training, the first OSS trainees emerged with sky-high morale, eager for their first mission.

Operational Group A, or Company A, four Italian-speaking groups, was the first OG contingent trained at Area F by Col. Lucius Rucker, one of the original Fort Benning paratroop instructors. This group arrived at OSS Station X, near Algiers, in late August 1943. The OG camp took over a former private beach community called Club des Pins, where the OGs lived in pup tents.[4] The nearby British SOE had established a base, codenamed Massingham, consisting of a training school, a parachute school, and communications facilities.

Col. Serge Obolensky supervised the program of the Italian unit, whose mission was to assist resistance forces fighting the Germans, first in Corsica and Sardinia and later in Italy. Obolensky had been an officer in the Imperial Russian Army, and he immigrated to the United States after the revolution. In New York he married an Astor heiress and became the darling of the New York social set.

The OGs in Corsica worked with the local Maquis to help liberate the island and to harass the German 90th Panzer Division, retreating from Sardinia. An OG base in Ile Rousse and Bastia operated for nine months providing anchorage for U.S. and British boats, with the mission of capturing neighboring islands Capraia and Gorgona and reporting intelligence on enemy coastal shipping. Another Italian OG group jumped into southeast Italy to help recover Allied prisoners whom the Italians released upon their surrender on 8 September.

On 13 September, Colonel Obolensky led the OSS team that parachuted into Sardinia. Their principal mission was bringing the message to the Italian troops that Marshal Pietro Badoglio, who had succeeded Mussolini as prime minister, had surrendered. After his Sardinia mission, Obolensky transferred to the OG training camp at Brockhall Castle, in Northampton, England. There he commanded yet another OG contingent of two French and two Norwegian groups. They were all dropped into German-occupied France after the Normandy invasion.[5]

Company B, a group of OGs trained in Washington to go into France, arrived at Area X in February and March 1944. Maj. Alfred T. Cox commanded this group, which came under the tactical control of Special Projects Operations Project Center (SPOC). These were the OGs with whom I worked.

In early 1944, it became necessary to formalize the relationships between Supreme Headquarters Allied Expeditionary Forces (SHAEF) in London and AFHQ in North Africa, for support and control of resistance forces in all parts of France. It was agreed that overall authority would reside with the former, but responsibility for southern France would be delegated through Special Forces Headquarters (SFHQ) to AFHQ, and specifically to SPOC Algiers, formally established on 1 May. In matters of policy, SPOC was to receive direction from SHAEF through SFHQ. Operationally, it was to function also under SHAEF but through the agency of SFHQ.

Until this centralization of control, OSS, through its Special Operations branch SO/North Africa, had a quid pro quo arrangement with French army headquarters in Algiers that initially provided the services of a limited number of French officers and enlisted men. In return, SO undertook to increase its capacity to provide paramilitary and parachute training for French army personnel.

The Maquis needed support for their guerrilla actions against the German occupation. Although they received varying degrees of help from the local population, they frequently needed essential supplies such as radios, and especially weapons and ammunition. The teams of Allied agents who parachuted in to the Maquis met a crucial need.

With few exceptions, American SO personnel in Algiers were not fluent in French, nor were they equipped to operate under cover with false papers, blending in to French folkways. Thus, it was felt that SO operations before D-Day could be performed most effectively by Frenchmen. Originally, about one hundred Frenchmen were recruited and trained in Algiers for work as SO agents in France. After they were made available to SPOC, another contingent of two hundred followed. In addition, six French-speaking OGs and twenty-five Jedburgh teams sent from London came under the tactical control of SPOC, as did the SO packing station in Algiers. An Air Operations Section was created to work with the bomber group that provided the airlift for body and supply drops from North Africa.

SPOC, to which I had been assigned, was located on the grounds of Villa Magnol. Despite the complexity of the organizational chains of command and the differing political agendas of the three Allied powers in waging the war, SPOC proved to be a remarkable success. American, British, and French intelligence officers worked together effectively under pressure to support resistance forces and, thereby, contribute significantly to the military campaign against the Germans. Statistics on SPOC's achievements are detailed in this chapter.[6]

During my search through the many boxes of declassified OSS records at the National Archives, a stroke of luck led me to this chart. While organization charts as a rule make dull reading, this one struck me like an electric shock, bringing back vivid memories of the thirty-one American officers with whom I worked in the SPOC Quonset huts. The American contingent accounted for

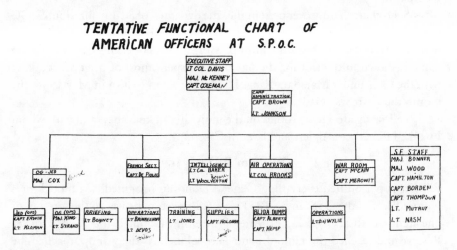

This is a flowchart for the group with whom I worked in SPOC Quonset huts.

Quonset huts, Villa Magnol

roughly one-third of the total SPOC staff. Col. William Davis was head of the American staff. His British counterpart was Col. John Anstey, an officer of Special Operations Executive and a former director of the Imperial Tobacco Company.

Such charts hardly ever present the true dynamics of an organization. SPOC was anything but a rigid array of static boxes, and people were moved around within the structure to meet the most pressing needs. For example, although my name is shown in the slot for the Jedburghs, I spent most of my time working with the OGs under Maj. Sam King. I had reported in to him in May 1944, the month the chart was made.[7]

Following are a few profiles on the individuals I knew best and with whom I worked directly in Algiers and later in Caserta.

William P. Davis Jr.

Bill Davis personified everything General Donovan imagined as a model for a senior officer of the OSS. In his 1931 class at Princeton, he was in the top four of one hundred ROTC graduates. After Princeton, he joined the Field Artillery Reserve and reached the rank of lieutenant colonel. As the war approached, he attended the Fort Leavenworth Command and General Staff School and graduated first in his class. Donovan would also have appreciated his social status and family background—son of a proper Philadelphia attorney and grandson of an Episcopal bishop.

Davis was a key figure at various stages of my military career, first in Algiers and then in Italy, where I continued to serve under him in Caserta. As a junior officer, on occasion I found him somewhat intimidating. I first encountered his stern, no-nonsense attitude when I approached him for a special favor, as we shall see.

Later, toward the end of his service in Operations in Caserta, Davis became disgusted with the bureaucratic atmosphere of that headquarters and the rivalries between SO and SOE. The personal vendettas and organizational environment so offended his action-oriented personality that he readily accepted transfer to the Far East. By this time, the war in Italy was reaching its final stages.

C. Martin Wood Jr.

Another product of Philadelphia's Main Line, Princeton, and the Field Artillery Reserve was Charles Martin Wood Jr. He was Bill Davis's junior by eight years, graduating from Princeton in 1939. Wood served as a reserve officer in Pennsylvania's 28th Division, from which he was called to active duty in 1941. He received his artillery training at Fort Sill and served there as an artillery instructor. While at Sill, Wood was ordered to report to OSS headquarters in Washington. After his OSS training, he was assigned to SPOC in Algiers. Subsequently he followed Davis to Caserta, where he served as his deputy in the Operations Section. Wood and I worked closely together there, until he was transferred to Washington. After that I replaced him as acting chief of Special Operations.

Stewart L. McKenney

Fortunately for me, I also served in Algiers under Davis's deputy in SPOC, Stewart McKenney, who, despite his regular Army background, was more approachable and easygoing than Davis. Stewart, a graduate of West Point, was assigned to the OSS in November 1943. After an initial assignment in London, he was sent to Algiers to aid in the organization of SPOC as executive officer to Davis. McKenney's orders included a special mandate to oversee the complicated relationships between SHAEF London and AFHQ Algiers. Once the SPOC was established, he frequently took over command of the organization because of Davis's heavy travel schedule. After the campaign in southern France ended, McKenney transferred to G-3 Special Operations AFHQ in Italy, where he was promoted to lieutenant colonel. The friendship we had formed in Algiers was strengthened in Caserta, when Stewart became one of my principal contacts in the daily AFHQ staff deliberations on strategy for support of the various partisan groups operating behind enemy lines.

Later in his distinguished Army career, General McKenney drew upon his OSS experience in assignments specializing in intelligence and Special Forces operations.

Samuel C. King

In contrast to Davis, Wood, and McKenney, Sam King had come into the Army as a private, with a background in the real estate and insurance businesses. Volunteering for parachute training at Fort Benning, he rose rapidly to the rank of major and was transferred to OSS Washington in June 1943, first as an OG recruiting officer and then as executive officer under Col. Russell Livermore. He arrived in Algiers just before I did, taking up his duties at SPOC. Soon after Victory in Europe (VE) Day, King was assigned to OSS Kunming and there again worked with his friend Al Cox.

Alfred T. Cox

Al Cox had majored in civil engineering at Lehigh University, where he excelled not only as a strong and agile athlete (captain of the football team and co-captain of baseball) but also as president of his class in his last two years and as a member of Phi Beta Kappa. OSS recruited Cox when he was an instructor of guerrilla warfare at the Infantry School at Fort Benning. At Area F in Washington, he played a key role in training and organizing the first OGs. From Area X in Algiers, he led the first of the OG teams sent to Corsica to carry out raids on the Italian coast, displaying the kind of leadership that inspired his men throughout his military career. Later he led Mission Lehigh, the final OG team in southern France, dropping into the Ardèche Department to aid the resistance movement there and coordinate operations of the OG sections in the Rhone River west-bank region.[8]

At the end of the war in Europe, OSS personnel were asked what they would choose as their next assignment, either in or out of the agency. It is typical of the commitment of such men as Davis and Cox that they both elected to transfer to OSS China. Cox was transferred to that command almost immediately after his Algiers service.

Kenneth Baker

A native of Vermont, Baker was a psychology professor at Ohio State University and an officer in the U.S. Army Reserve at the outbreak of war. Like Davis, Baker was a graduate of the Fort Leavenworth Command and General Staff School. The OSS recruited him for his professional skills in the then relatively new field of psychological warfare. A few days after Pearl Harbor, General Donovan summoned Baker and D. C. Hayden, a former vice governor of the Philippines, to his office. He informed them that he wanted them to set up the OSS training schools.

Maj. Alfred T. Cox

In preparation for this task, Baker was sent to Munn's school in England, a facility specializing in psychological warfare. He and Baker, in consultation with the British, developed the original curriculum for future OSS operatives in the camps around Washington. In late summer 1944, when the Germans were yielding to the Allied offensive in southern France, Baker moved to the military frontline to head up SPOC's advance unit Special Forces Unit 4 (SFU4), representing SPOC with the Seventh Army and the 6th Army Group. After VE Day, he administered the SPOC debriefing report.

William Hollohan

Of all the officers shown on the SPOC chart, William Hollohan stands out as the figure whose ultimate fate has created the greatest mystery and controversy. In private life he was a Securities and Exchange Commission lawyer who served in a

National Guard unit in New York. Like most of the other American SPOC officers, Hollohan went from Algiers to Italy, where he led a team dropped in to support the resistance. We will come back in chapter 4 to the story of his disappearance and conflicting theories on what happened to the Hollohan mission.

Despite their different backgrounds, these American officers shared certain traits essential to leadership. They courted and even thrived on the hazards of OSS missions and the opportunity to prove themselves. Shaped from the same mold as General Donovan, they chose to take part in the most crucial military actions, usually involving the greatest danger.

In Algiers, I had been transferred from an operational to an intelligence staff status, as we have seen. In contrast to my time in Cairo, where I felt a bit guilty about the easy life, my duties now were definitely more meaningful. I became fully engaged in the logistics of preparing OG teams for their missions. Thus I was involved in selecting sites for personnel and supply drops, providing maps of local terrain and data on partisan forces as well as enemy strength, and collecting clothing, medical supplies, and other gear that the teams needed.

By the time of my arrival, the other staff officers had developed various standard operating procedures (SOPs) and daily routines that I, as the new guy, had to learn how to follow. Every morning on their arrival, the French officers shook hands with everyone in the hut. British custom was observed in visits to the canteen for tea, at eleven in the morning and four in the afternoon. A delightful group of women from the FANY corps performed clerical duties; I had first encountered them in Cairo. The SPOC staff never lost sight of the serious nature of our task, yet a spirit of jovial camaraderie prevailed.

Initially I was billeted in the officer Quonset huts adjacent to Villa Magnol. Later I was assigned a small, spartan room in downtown Algiers. Its only memorable feature was the hordes of cockroaches that I dealt with by setting the legs of my bed in bowls of water. Each day I commuted by Jeep up the long, winding road to Magnol.

Much to my surprise, one day my former roommate Bill Underwood turned up. He had finished his training in Washington along with his friend Winthrop Rutherford, and they had been assigned an SO mission into the southwest of France, near the Pyrenees. Both men were quite a bit older than I, and neither seemed altogether fit for the rigors of an SO mission. Yet they had completed parachute training and were ready to be dropped into France, while I was still doing staff work involving no risks at all. I felt some pangs of guilt about my desk-bound existence.[9]

With my troubled conscience I went to see Col. Bill Davis, my commanding officer, to ask permission to take jump training. In his customary stern manner he refused, pointing out that my status had been switched to intelligence.

My deputy, William Underwood

Thus I had no mission that would justify jump training. After this brief meeting, my conscience was eased by having at least made an effort, and I was relieved that I would not be leaping out of a plane. I happily carried on my duties with the OGs, as we began sending one team after another into southern France.

When most of the teams had been successfully dropped, Davis himself parachuted into France to evaluate the situation in the field. As soon as he left, his more flexible deputy, Major McKenney, summoned me and said he would approve my request for jump training. Now I was on the spot. I had to accept his offer or show myself to be chicken.

A few days later, I was enrolled in a one-day session to learn the basics. At Blida, the airfield dedicated to Allied intelligence missions, we practiced in a British Halifax built with an accommodating round hole in the floor of its fuse-lage. Parachutists sat on the edge of this hole and, at a signal from the dispatcher, pushed themselves over the edge. We jumped a number of times from a simula-tor plane, at a height of about ten feet off the ground. Other basics we were taught included maneuvering the chute during descent, hitting the ground the right way, and gathering up the chute before the wind caught it. These instruc-tions were not particularly daunting, especially since we did not have to stand in the door and push ourselves outside the plane, as in a C-47.

Even so, I spent a fairly restless night before rising early the next day to face the real thing. When we arrived at the field, we learned that no British planes were available and so we would have to jump from an American C-47, for which we had had no training. Not a welcome turn of events! But somehow, when the moment came, I managed to hurl myself out the door and enjoy the thrill that comes when your chute actually billows out. That was my one and only jump, for Colonel Davis returned from France and I could not tell him that his deputy had countermanded his order. But many years later, I was seated next to Bill Davis at a dinner and had the pleasure of letting him know that he had been overruled and that I had jumped while he was off in France. He seemed to get quite a kick from this "only in the OSS" kind of story.

In anticipation of the invasions of Normandy and southern France, a group of Maquis had begun to assemble in a natural Alpine fortress, a four-hundred-square-mile isolated wilderness called the Vercors, in the southeast. More than thirty-five hundred Maquis stalwarts, joined by some OSS and SOE liaison officers and an Operational Group of fifteen men, were preparing to make this a stronghold capable of staving off a German military onslaught. The defenders on the ground thought that the highest authorities in Allied headquarters had endorsed their defense strategy for the region, whereas in fact their carefully conceived plan had been lost in London's administrative bureaucracy.

After the Normandy invasion was launched, the Vercors defenders, expecting to be supplied with heavy weapons including mortars and antitank guns, along with Allied airborne support, continued to pursue their plans for denying their territory to the Germans. They even proclaimed the "Free Republic of the Vercors." Indeed, they did manage a surprising defense against the first German assault on 13 June 1944.

However, after that initial battle they received only rifles and automatic weapons. No mortars, antitank guns, or airborne troops. The Germans mounted a second major offense, with heavy bombing and strafing as a prelude to an assault by twenty-two thousand German soldiers. The result was a horrible massacre of the civilian population in the Vercors region. Although OSS officers were able to effect the escape of some of the Maquis leaders, a counterattack led by the OG team failed and a bloodbath ensued, with slaughter of huge numbers of the civilian populace, including children. Some of the victims were hung, and the bodies of others were suspended on butchers' meat hooks.

The disaster soured French attitudes toward the British and American Special Forces. In the midst of considerable scapegoating about the cause of the tragedy among various factions in London headquarters, the commander of French resistance forces, Gen. Joseph Pierre Koenig, insisted that he be given some control over both OSS and SOE operations. General Eisenhower, recognizing the validity of his argument, granted his request. A structure for integrating French and Anglo-American Special Operations was instituted. About the only positive comment to be made on the Vercors tragedy is that it caused the Germans to divert a sizable force from their main military objectives.[10]

The Allied leaders had begun discussing plans for the invasion of southern France at the Tehran conference in November 1943. The original codename Anvil was switched to Dragoon as a security precaution, shortly before the actual invasion. As Churchill wrote in his memoir, the proposal to mount an invasion of southern France led to the first important divergence between the United States and Great Britain on high strategy. Originally, its British proponents had conceived the invasion as a feint, or just a means to keep German divisions in southern France from joining the anticipated battles after Normandy. The Americans had pressed for a large-scale attack by ten divisions, and at Tehran Stalin had supported this strategy. Churchill signed on reluctantly.

In the end, the three leaders agreed to launch Overlord and Anvil simultaneously, as soon as Rome had been captured. But Rome did not fall until 4 June, a long five months after the overly optimistic projections at Tehran and only one day before Overlord.[11] Because of a shortage of landing craft and the time required to move troops from the Italian campaign to the south of France, Anvil was launched two months after Overlord.

A major strategic issue that Churchill, Roosevelt, and the top military commands debated was the allocation of manpower between the campaigns in southern France and Italy. It was apparent that substantial numbers of troops fighting in Italy would have to be diverted to support the major drive of troops in southern France and fighting eastward from Normandy under General Eisenhower. However, shipping seasoned troops from Italy would have serious repercussions for that campaign. Both senior British commanders, Gen. Maitland Wilson, supreme commander in the Mediterranean, and Gen. Harold Alexander, commanding general of the 15th Army Group in Italy, came finally to the opinion that the wisest course would be to forego the Anvil plan altogether, in order to finish off the Germans in Italy.

Ultimately, the Alliance decided in favor of the U.S.-backed initiative, and planning for the invasion of southern France proceeded. It should be noted, however, that as late as 6 August 1944, only ten days before Anvil/Dragoon was launched, Churchill was pleading the case against the Riviera invasion and in favor of the Atlantic coast of Brittany, south of the Cherbourg peninsula at St. Nazaire. In a letter to Harry Hopkins for FDR's attention, Churchill argued that the Atlantic would present a far less formidable invasion site than the "well fortified Riviera coast." In Hopkins's reply, he countered that an invasion of Brittany was not an option, mainly because of its "insurmountable" supply problems.[12]

Preparations for Operation Dragoon continued apace. A large force, totaling 450,000 soldiers including the Seventh Army under command of Lt. Gen. Alexander Patch, was assembled for the attack. It consisted of seven French and three U.S. divisions, together with a mixed American and British airborne division. About 250,000 of the French contingent consisted of troops from France's colonies. The three American divisions had been taken from Gen. Mark Clark's Fifth Army in Italy, while four of the French divisions and a large part of the Allied air forces had been taken from General Alexander's command, cutting seriously into Allied strength in Italy.

When the invading force swarmed ashore at the chic Riviera beaches between Toulon and Cannes on 16 August, they suffered only light casualties, largely because of detailed data on German defensive fortifications that OSS intelligence had provided. Prime Minister and former First Lord of the Admiralty Churchill observed the landing from the British destroyer *Kimberley.* In hindsight, it has become clear that although the southern France invasion was successful in driving out the Germans, the two-month delay in launching it was a costly tactical error. Furthermore, the diversion of troops from the Italian campaign, along with a parallel diversion of British troops to Greece, seriously crippled the Allied drive up the Italian peninsula. However, the contribution of OSS teams operating behind the lines proved the value of the underlying concept and won the respect of military commanders.

The OG teams were grouped according to language capability; there were eight sections of French speakers, three Italian, two German, and one mixed French-Italian. All had received advanced infantry training in addition to guerrilla warfare, mountain operations, and parachute training. Typical OG teams were composed of two officers and thirteen enlisted men, one being the wireless operator. The five specific missions assigned to each unit were

1. Cut and harass enemy lines of communication
2. Attack vital enemy installations
3. Organize and train local resistance elements
4. Boost morale and effort of local resistance elements
5. Furnish intelligence to the Allied armies

From 8 June to 1 September, ten French, three Italian, and one mixed OG teams were dropped into southern France. Table 1 (opposite) shows their names, the composition of each team, and their schedule. Those missing in action are listed (1), along with those killed in action (5) and wounded (23). Altogether, those numbers represent 16 percent of the 27 officers and 155 enlisted men who were dropped.

Six OG teams were dropped into their target areas before the Alice team parachuted into the Drome region on 6 August, just ten days before the Anvil/Dragoon

Table 1: Operational Groups
Unit Operations

Name	Date	Department	Composition O.	Composition EM	MIA	KIA	W
1. Emily	6/8	Cantal-Lot	2	13 (French)			1
2. Justine	6/28	Vercors	2	13 (French)	1		1
3. Louise	7/17	Ardeche	2	13 (French)		2	5
4. Betsy	7/25	Ardeche	2	11 (French)			2
5. Ruth	8/3	Basses-Alpes	2	13 (French)			2
6. Pat	8/6	Tarn	2	13 (French)		2	2
7. Alice	8/6	Drome	2	13 (French)			
8. Peg	8/11	Aude	2	13 (French)		1	2
9. Justine (1V)	8/11	Ardeche	0	1 (French)			
10. Nancy	8/12	Hautes-Alpes	2	13 (Italian)			
11. Lehigh	8/24	Ardeche	3	5 (French)			1
12. Helen	8/29	Ardeche	2	13 (Italian)			
13. Lafayette	8/29	Ardeche	2	12 (Italian)			6
14. Williams	9/1	Ardeche	2	9 (mixed)			1
14			26	155	1	5	23*

* Approximately ten of the wounded were injuries received on the combat jump.

landing (see Table 1). Each has its own unique story. I have chosen to tell the Alice story here, mainly because it typifies the OG experience but also because of my own incidental involvement.

One of the enlisted men on this team was Cpl. Francis I. G. Coleman (always known as Fig), two years behind me at Princeton, where we had known each other slightly. I did not know he was in Algiers and heard the following story from him only after the war. On the night of 6 August 1944, the Alice team assembled in a glade of trees next to Blida airfield. There a representative from headquarters was to meet them for a final briefing on all the crucial information. The plan was that they would rendezvous with the Maquis in the Drome region, near the town of Montelimar. The HQ officer was to update them on enemy troop movements in the region, the latest reports on Maquis forces, and strategies for attacking their assigned targets. The success of the whole mission and the well-being of each team member depended on the accuracy of the briefing that this official gave.

When the command car from HQ drove up, Fig was astonished and dismayed to see that I was the officer who emerged. Instead of a senior ranking official, he was being shortchanged with a lowly lieutenant who had none of the experience or credentials for such a crucial assignment. Fortunately, Fig kept his concerns to himself rather than alarming his teammates. The rendezvous came off as planned, and Alice went on to achieve most of its assigned objectives.

Based on team members' reports for the OG debriefing in Grenoble, I have since learned the following details.[13] The Alice team departed Blida airfield in a Halifax at 2130 hours, heading for a drop zone twenty-eight kilometers due east of Montelimar. Flying was graded "excellent," with an efficient and cooperative crew. From the navigator's seat came constant encouraging reports of good parachuting weather, further boosting morale. The trip was spent just talking things over, sleeping, and thinking. "Everyone was tense, eager," reads one report. Although the length of the drop zone was reported to be short, the drop itself went well, with the two lieutenants, Ralph Barnard and Donald Meeks, each leading a "stick" of parachutists. All landings were "effected safely with only slight injuries." The reception was "excellent, well organized," with three friendly fires burning and "scattered Frenchmen awaiting our arrival with curiosity." Three men with slight foot injuries were taken to a nearby hospital for x-rays and treatment. Maquis officers and men served wine in one of the peasant houses. The chutes and equipment were collected and stored safely, and the team departed for their hideout in the hills. There, after something of a night march, they were fed and quartered at 0400.

Later that morning, the two officers went off to locate the Maquis commanders in the area; the radio men established contact with Algiers, and other section members talked with the Maquis on the general situation. "Morale was excellent everywhere." Maquis commandant Le Grand was located the next day, and arrangements were made to move the section northwest of the Drome River near the Rhone, where "we could begin our job." Most of that day was spent locating transportation, loading equipment, and preparing for the move. The men who had been treated in the hospital rejoined the section, and "people in the town were glad to see us."

On 10, 11, and 12 August, the Alice team moved through the Drome valley to the small town of Les Fouquets, where they set up headquarters in a farmhouse, made radio contact with Algiers, and met Lieutenant Kirsch, leader of a fifteen-man Maquis group with whom they would work. On their way, they saw the damage the retreating Germans had done in burning villages and farms. They observed the tremendous boost in the morale of the people on seeing American soldiers. From their new headquarters, they could see Valence and Chabeuil, site of a German airfield protected by artillery.

Coleman (left) and Richard Condon

On the night of the twelfth, the two OG lieutenants, three of the sergeants, and Lieutenant Kirsch conducted a reconnaissance of a strategic bridge on Route Nationale 538 and a high-tension power line between two seventy-foot towers. They narrowly missed being observed by French militia, in a truck disguised as a Red Cross ambulance. That evening, a ten-man group succeeded in blowing up both towers and shutting off all power along this line.

A second group set up an ambush at the bridge on RN 538, where for nearly eight hours they stayed in position to attack, but there was no traffic. They returned to a nearby village to bed down for what was left of the night.

On the afternoon of 13 August, while Alice was climbing up to their base in the mountains, they witnessed the American Air Corps bombing the town of Crest. The next day, a Maquis delegation came to ask them to reassure the townspeople that the bombing was a mistake and would not be repeated. Upon arriving in Crest, the team was greeted by a "very down-hearted and somewhat belligerent" group of people. About one-fourth of the town had been destroyed; thirty-eight people had been killed, and one hundred wounded. Lieutenants Barnard and Meeks talked with the people, visited the wounded in the hospital, and assured everyone that such a horrible mistake would not happen again. (In fact, the Air Corps was evidently trying to bomb the railroad bridge that the Maquis had already destroyed on 6 July.)

On 15 August, Alice received orders from Maquis headquarters to blow the bridge on RN 538. At 0300 the whole section left the base in the hills in two vehicles, one a Model A Ford coal burner carrying the demolitions and the other a little Renault for personnel. Although mechanical problems with each car caused delays, the team reached the target area at 0930, and the demolition squad began preparing the charges. Being of stone construction, the bridge required 125 pounds of C-2. After it was blown, Lieutenants Barnard and Meeks inspected the damage and found that it was a perfect demolition job.

Alice now moved back up the mountain toward their base, stopping at a friendly farmer's house for lunch. They saw the Air Corps bomb Valence while German antiaircraft fire brought down three C-47s. One of the three crews bailed out, and Alice team members went searching for them, trying to reach them before the Germans. But it was the Maquis who rescued the two crew members and brought them to Alice the next day. Alice then radioed headquarters a report on their status.

On 16 August, the team moved down from the valley to an abandoned schoolhouse in Ourches, where they were close to a German command post. Before they could carry out a plan to attack it, the Germans moved out. But two days later, they learned that some twenty Germans and five trucks loaded with supplies were at a schoolyard in the nearby village of Montmeyran, preparing to move out at nightfall. A hastily arranged plan was devised, calling for the Maquis to proceed first through the village, providing protection against the possible arrival of Germans from a nearby camp where six thousand troops were stationed. The Maquis were also given the job of cutting telephone lines that connected to this camp. The attack team of eight Alice members and three Maquis crammed into two small cars to move undetected into the village.

In the words of the report, "As is often the case, however, tactical plans were forgotten and the two cars roared into the village, one behind the other, in true gangster fashion." Although the screams of mothers calling their children off the streets quickly announced the presence of the Americans, the team managed to reach the schoolyard before the Germans knew what was happening. German soldiers standing by the trucks were cut down as they tried to escape into the schoolhouse. One German opened fire from a second-story window.

Alice Team with Marquis resistance force in Ourches

With his machine pistol, he easily could have wiped out the entire team, but, fortunately, his aim was poor. Maquis lieutenant Kirsch took care of the loaded supply trucks with well-placed Gammon grenades.

The villagers disappeared from the streets, with the exception of a few Maquis girls who served heroically as scouts. For about half an hour, it was nip and tuck as a pitched battle was waged, but the Alice section and the Maquis finally began to win.

The Germans, many of them killed or wounded, ceased any organized fighting. Alice dispersed back into the mountains. Lieutenant Kirsch remained in town until he was certain that all Alice team members had left. On assembling back at camp, the team realized that except for minor shrapnel wounds that three of them had sustained, they had come through the operation practically unscathed. Villagers later reported that sixteen Germans were killed, an unknown number wounded, and four trucks and one command car destroyed.

After the raid, the villagers all fled to the mountains, fearing the German reprisals that always followed in a village that the Maquis attacked. Strangely, though, Germans never returned in sufficient numbers. They had an exaggerated idea of how many Americans were in the vicinity, it was learned subsequently.

On 20 August, the Alice team prepared to set up an ambush on their main target, National Route 7, known as the Route Napoleon. They observed many long convoys moving north hastily, but they were too large for a small unit to attack. At dawn on 21 August, a lone truck with a full load of German soldiers moved up the road, and Alice destroyed it with grenades and small-arms fire. The Germans managed to set up a machine gun in a nearby building, but the team quickly dispersed up the hillside and none were hit. An estimated thirty Germans were killed and a few others wounded in this action.

Later that same morning, advance elements of the U.S. 36th Division overran Alice. Three war correspondents greeted the team some time after that, representing United Press, the *London Times,* and the *Washington Times.* They had lunch together while Alice rejoiced at the Americans' arrival. At this same moment the German retreat was well under way, but their artillery fire narrowly missed some of the Alice team members in the schoolyard in Crest. People in the Drome region continued to fear the Germans' return and their desperate earth-scorching tactics. Meanwhile, Alice lieutenants searched in vain for Special Forces officers in the military commands to whom they could report. After several days, Algiers radio ordered the team to move to a Maquis camp near Grenoble, where they awaited the arrival of other OG teams to establish a headquarters.

The OG contingent of 27 officers and 155 enlisted men accomplished amazing results in their harassment of enemy forces, as revealed by the following statistics.

Germans killed	461
Germans wounded	467
German prisoners	10,021
Vehicles destroyed	33
Bridges destroyed	32
Power lines and cables destroyed	11
Roads mined	17
Aircraft shot down	3
Trains destroyed	2
Locomotives destroyed	3

Supreme Allied Commander Gen. Dwight D. Eisenhower acknowledged the importance of the French resistance when he said, "The disruption of enemy rail communications, the harassing of German road moves and increasing strain put on the German . . . internal security services throughout occupied Europe by the organized forces of resistance played a very considerable part in our complete and final victory."[14] In fact, OSS and SOE operations enabled the surrender of some thirty thousand Germans in southern France, preventing them from joining the Nazi forces opposing the Allies in Normandy.

After VE Day, Major Cox convened all the OG teams for a debriefing in Grenoble. The report of that meeting, together with the mission reports of each of the fourteen teams, provides an excellent historical account of the period. The major purposes of the exercise were to record lessons learned from these unprecedented operations and to draw conclusions for future Special Operations. It was the OGs' self-critique of what they had accomplished and what could have been done more effectively.

Not surprisingly, in the Grenoble debriefing report, opinion differed from one team to another according to circumstances. On one point, however, there was unanimous agreement: "The teams should have been put into France much earlier than they were. Every day spent in training the Maquis brought increased dividends in their combat effectiveness. After the Debarkation from the South, the advance of the Army was so rapid that the sections sent in after D-Day barely had a chance to get started on operations before they were over-run."[15] Some additional key findings follow.

1. Organization and discipline varied from little to very good, but the presence of regular Army officers and noncoms exerted positive influence in all cases.
2. Wherever the teams traveled among the general population, they were enthusiastically received and accorded excellent cooperation.
3. The FFI won praises for doing a fine job in administering to the Maquis forces. Normally there was plenty of food for all.
4. The FFI could have been more effective if it had focused on continual guerrilla warfare tactics instead of trying to concentrate huge Maquis forces into an army for the liberation of large towns. Many good targets for guerrilla attacks were neglected in the last months, in favor of more spectacular projects.
5. Political animosities between various parties often hampered operations, and became acute in some places that were now completely liberated.

French officers sent in on missions tended quickly to lose their identities as Allied leaders and become French political chiefs instead. The employment of only American and British personnel in the coordination of Maquis efforts could have prevented many of these difficulties.

In January 2003, I received an email message from a paratroop reserve officer in the French army, François Heilbronn. He was trying to track down information on his great uncle François Klotz, an OSS agent. Klotz was killed soon after being dropped on 28 June 1944 into the Vaucluse, near the town of Sainte-Tulle on the Durance River. Having learned that I had signed Klotz's citation for the posthumous award of the Silver Star, Heilbronn had located me through an Internet search. For sixty years, Klotz's family had been seeking in vain to determine the exact circumstances of his death and the location of a gravesite. Heilbronn and I began an email correspondence that, although it left unresolved some questions, made me aware of how some families strive, still today, to honor the memory of relatives who fought in the resistance, along with American Special Operations forces. Using as sources Klotz's award recommendation and other declassified records in the archives, the following story about Operation Mercenary can be told.[16]

Klotz was the head of a six-man team to take charge of the Bernard radio circuit, consisting of French resistance members trained for guerrilla warfare. The Gestapo was making a concentrated effort to extinguish resistance in this area, and the French agent who had previously headed this group had been killed in April. Thus, the Mercenary mission involved exceptional risk.

After the drop, the team was received by a committee of five men headed by the wireless operator Laurent, but almost immediately they encountered a German-manned roadblock and were greatly outnumbered. Klotz and three of his team were killed almost instantly, while Laurent escaped. Suspicions about the wireless operator's reliability had been raised even while the mission was in the planning stages. Today it seems likely that Laurent was a collaborationist who betrayed Klotz and his team. Moreover, despite extensive searches in the area, no gravesite has been found for Klotz and the others who sacrificed their lives in the cause of liberation.

As we have already seen, the OGs recognized the need for debriefing. Similarly, the leaders of SPOC undertook a debriefing operation at Special Forces Unit 4, in Avignon. Whereas the OG effort focused mainly on tactics, at SPOC there was a broader, more strategic emphasis.

During the summer of 1944, SPOC infiltrated a total of 212 Americans into southern France. Of these, 9 were SO agents, 21 were Jedburghs, and 182 were OGs formed into fourteen combat units. During and after the Anvil invasion, SFU4 represented SPOC with the Seventh Army. Its purpose was to coordinate the activities of the several SPOC teams with the Maquis, the Seventh Army, and the Sixth Army Group. It also provided a central wireless link between the field and SPOC Algiers. Agents sent situation reports, supply requests, and other communications to Algiers via the SFU4 link. During the last two weeks of August and into early September, when action against the enemy had virtually ceased in most of southern France, SFU4 fulfilled a crucial communications role. Soon after the fall of Lyon to the Seventh Army, SPOC and SFU4 were liquidated.

Some of the main points that the SPOC report stressed follow.[17]

1. The SFU4 Avignon debriefing base was set up too late, long after many agents were prepared and waiting to make their reports. OSS

(London) and SOE had transferred many to new assignments even before the Avignon base was established.

2. In addition to the debriefing, SFU4 became involved in several "extracurricular" matters because it was the only U.S. military unit between Lyon and Marseilles. Baker, as senior officer, had to deal with issues such as continuing calls from eastern-sector Maquis for operational equipment and assistance.

3. Operations personnel criticized the assigning of priorities to targets. SFU4 admitted a tendency to go for those "most easily attacked"— which probably meant that the Germans considered them less important. More important targets were likely to be better guarded.

4. Intelligence on targets was sometimes outdated.

5. Briefings on political situations in areas of operation were sometimes inadequate. Teams were directed to stay clear of politics before they departed for a mission, but in the field, politics were a major factor in dictating operations. Therefore, teams should have been warned in advance that it would be hard to avoid becoming embroiled.

6. Whereas Jedburgh teams tended to be highly individualistic, aggressive, tough, and ready to take things in their own hands when their superiors were found wanting, Baker found the OGs well disciplined and organized during their entire time in France.

7. Resupply operations were very irregular. Agents' personal belongings often failed to arrive at the time of initial drop.

A big problem for SPOC and SFU4, before they disbanded, was the extraordinarily hostile attitude of General de Gaulle toward the Frenchmen who had volunteered to work with the British and French teams supporting the Maquis. In a complete reversal from the general's position when the French volunteers were first being recruited for these assignments, de Gaulle came to regard them almost as traitors for operating under direction of a foreign government. This was an early foreshadowing of how difficult an ally Le Grand Charles would prove to be.

The war in Italy had begun a year before the invasion of southern France. The first Allied assault on Italy was the landing of one American and one British army in Sicily on 9 July 1943. General Donovan went ashore with this landing and personally directed the OSS unit, consisting of two officers and eight enlisted men.[18] The Salerno landing took place on 9 September, and this began the long and difficult struggle to drive the Axis off the peninsula. Realizing that the Germans would ultimately be driven out of France, and recognizing the challenge posed by the Italian campaign, AFHQ moved from Algiers to Caserta. On 7 July 1944, the headquarters of the 2677th Regiment also moved to Caserta.

A memorandum dated 16 August 1944, entitled "Reorganization of OSS Activities in the Mediterranean Theater," details the structural changes related to moving the bulk of OSS personnel from North Africa. Our new structure would consist of three main groups and a headquarters.

> Company A, with Col. Edward Gamble in command, would move its forward element to southern France, with the staging area for this movement based in Caserta and the rear echelon remaining in Algiers, until all personnel were dropped into France.
>
> Company D, with Captain Suhling in command, would be located in north central Italy. Its headquarters, in Siena, would operate exclusively for Allied Armies in Italy (AAI), including the Fifth and Eighth Armies.
>
> The Balkan area would be covered by OSS strength in Bari, Istanbul, and Cairo, under the command of Col. John E. Toulmin.
>
> The headquarters of OSS Mediterranean Theater of Operations would be located at San Leucio, adjacent to AFHQ Caserta. A small intelligence group would also be located near Rome.

Additional organizational changes provided for dispersing Company C in Corsica, placing the four OSS stations in North Africa under direct control of OSS Washington, placing the Air Resupply Detachment operating at Brindisi under control of OSS headquarters MEDTO, and placing all in-theater OG personnel in the 2671st Special Reconnaissance Battalion under the command of Col. Russell Livermore, as a part of OSS MEDTO headquarters.[19]

While these organizational moves were being developed at senior levels in Washington and in the field, I was fully occupied with my job in SPOC. The move of 2677th Regimental headquarters to Caserta took place more than a month before the Anvil/Dragoon invasion, and SPOC had a full load of work in dropping teams into southern France. The Germans were still strongly entrenched in most of France. As shown in Table 1, the first of the OG teams was dropped on 8 June and the fourteenth on 1 September.

As the Allied offensive in France gained ground, and after all the OG teams had taken off on their missions, the workload for staffers such as me eased up. I could relax a bit and enjoy some of the attractions of Algiers and the surrounding countryside. Along with a couple of friends, Arthur Cox of the Yugoslav desk and Al Ulmer of the Austrian desk, I made several trips to the beaches along the coast. Arthur was greatly indebted to me because I loaned him the snappy Brooks Brothers Glen plaid suit that I had brought with me. He had shipped abroad with only rough outdoor clothing, suitable for the mountains of Yugoslavia. In Washington, I had been instructed to pack civilian gear in case an undercover mission came up, as well as my regular Army gear. Arthur wore my beautiful suit until it was nothing but threads, and he bought me a new one after the war.

We three had been involved in supporting operations, each in our respective area. In this interlude, we got to know some of the American women working in the Registry and R&A branches in Villa Magnol. Life was taking on a very pleasant complexion, but we knew that time was running out. My orders to proceed to Caserta came through on 21 September. Six days later, I was promoted to first lieutenant.

4

Caserta, 1944
22 September to 31 December 1944

The war in Italy, despite bloody battles and huge Allied troop losses, was regarded in some military circles as a diversion from the main assault on Germany. It even earned the inglorious and, in this author's view, totally unjustified epithet the Sideshow War. The Italian peninsula, nowhere more than 150 miles wide, posed complex problems for the Allies. Strategists in the high commands differed on the issue of invading Italy. Those in opposition argued that the rugged, mountainous terrain favored the German and Italian defenders, and that committing Allied troops to Italy would prevent their use in the main attack against the German homeland.[1]

The British were the principal advocates of the Italian campaign. Early in the North African hostilities, they had to stave off an Italian threat to seize the Suez Canal. Italian submarines, surface ships, and airplanes constantly threatened British shipping in the Mediterranean. The adventure into Greece, Mussolini's foolhardy and ultimately doomed initiative, had threatened the longstanding British interest there. The Italians represented a real menace to the British. At the Casablanca Conference in January 1943, Churchill dragged up his favorite argument for attacking the "soft underbelly of Europe" and ordered General Alexander to draw up plans for attacking Italy even while the North African campaign was in full swing.

Many American strategists, however, questioned the wisdom of invading Italy. The United States was seen to have less of a strategic interest in the area than the British. Moreover, the American public was less hostile than were the British to the Italians but regarded Mussolini's regime as a bunch of buffoons who at least knew how to make the trains run on time.

Ultimately, the United States joined forces with the British in the Italian campaign. But there always remained an unsettling ambiguity about Italy. Strategists recognized that the terrain up the entire boot gave an almost insurmountable advantage to the defenders by making it impossible to push them all the way up the peninsula. Short of that, there was no militarily "right" place in which to push the offensive to a conclusion. Partly by default, Rome came to be regarded as the symbolic goal of an Allied offensive. Indeed, its fall on 4 June 1944 represented the high point of the Italian campaign. After Rome, however, the Allies had no choice but to continue slogging away up the peninsula in a brutal campaign that cost thousands of lives.

The question of how to finish off this campaign came to involve a debate over one of Churchill's favorite strategies, focusing on the so-called Ljublana Gap, a pass northeast of Trieste. The prime minister and some of his advisers believed it would be possible to breach the Gothic Line, the series of formidable defenses built by the Wehrmacht, to defend the Po Valley, and from there swing east all the way over to the Istrian peninsula. Once there, the Ljublana Gap offered essential access to Austria and, ultimately, Vienna. However, to adopt such a strategy in light of the virtually impenetrable military obstacles required a tremendous leap of faith. The political motive behind this concept was the sealing off of the Istrian peninsula from occupation by Yugoslav forces and their Communist contagion.

Roosevelt and his military chiefs were never persuaded of the feasibility of this strategy. They argued that it was a deviation from the grand strategy the Allies had agreed on, that it would take too long and require more troops than could be made available, and that the American public would see it as a distraction from Overlord, in which so many American soldiers were involved.[2]

The origins of an American intelligence operation in Italy trace back to the winter of 1941, when David Bruce, later to become the legendary diplomat, was chief of the Secret Intelligence (SI) branch of the Coordinator of Intelligence (COI). Bruce had persuaded Earl Brennan, a former consular officer with whom he had served in Rome, to take over the Italian section of SI. Together, Bruce and Brennan developed a general plan for SI Italy and submitted it to General Donovan, who gave them a green light. Brennan recruited as the first member of his staff a twenty-two-year-old U.S. Army private, Max Corvo, who had grown up in Sicily. There he helped his father print an anti-Fascist newspaper. Upon coming to America with his family, he soon volunteered for the Army and began work on plans to recruit Italo-Americans for military intelligence purposes. After joining OSS, he adapted these ideas in an action plan for SI Italy. In January 1943, Corvo recruited another Sicilian American, Vincent Scamporino, who was sent to North Africa to head SI Italy under the direction of Colonel Eddy. Another early recruit was an attorney, Emilio Q. Daddario, a Wesleyan University football star who started as Corvo's assistant operations officer and moved on to key positions in SI Brindisi and, finally, in Switzerland with Allen Dulles.

As the time approached for the invasion of Sicily on 9 July 1943, SI had the most qualified pool of Italo-American personnel within OSS. Under Corvo's leadership, it played the lead OSS role in that campaign. General Donovan, setting the precedent he would follow in other operations, was personally in the vanguard of the invasion. He landed on the beach with the first assault and advanced inland with the infantry, manning a light machine gun.

Before the invasion, British navy officials had concocted an elaborate ruse, Operation Mincemeat, to confuse the Germans about where the Allies would attack. The scheme, conceived by Lt. Cdr. Ewen Montagu, consisted of planting plans for invasions of both Sardinia and Corsica, attached to a body disguised as a drowning victim from a downed Allied aircraft. A British submarine would slip the body into the sea off the Spanish coast, where currents would carry it ashore to be picked up by either Spanish authorities or German counterintelligence forces. They would relay the false plans up the chain of command, ultimately to Hitler. The Germans were almost completely taken in by the ruse and began arming for invasions of the two islands while diverting two of their armored divisions from the Russian front. Montagu's memoirs became the subject of a fictionalized version of the plot in a 1954 film, *The Man Who Never Was*. Admiral Jewell, who commanded the submarine that dropped the body off the Spanish coast, died in September 2004 at age ninety.

While the British were engaged in their scheming, the OSS was helping to shape another extraordinary espionage plot before the invasion. With OSS backing, the Office of Naval Intelligence and the assistant district attorney of New York negotiated a deal with the Mafia-controlled Murder Incorporated to collect intelligence from the Sicilian Mafia and help police the New York waterfront against Nazi spies and saboteurs. In exchange, New York mob boss Lucky Luciano, then behind bars, would be released from prison. Although documentary evidence on the value of any intelligence secured through this channel is limited, Luciano was released and deported from the United States the day after the war ended.

In Sicily, SI displayed its versatility by conducting a variety of operations, including tactical intelligence, line infiltration, counterintelligence, and psychological warfare. The first counterintelligence team that SI set up became a model for what became Counter Intelligence (X2). SI even mounted the kind of operation that later would have been conducted by Special Operations (SO) or the Operational Groups (OGs). They captured the Lipari Islands, turned them over to the American military government, and took fifty prisoners of war for interrogation.

The Allied liberation of Sicily signaled the end of Mussolini's corrupt regime that had ruled Italy for twenty-one years. Virtually the entire Italian fleet surrendered to the British in Malta. In Rome, King Victor Emmanuel, nearly the only supporter of il Duce, was forced by the advice of his Grand Council to realize that the attack on Sicily and the impending invasion of the mainland would inevitably result in the collapse of Italian resistance. The king and his counselors arranged for Mussolini's arrest and his internment on the island of Ponza. Marshal Pietro Badoglio, a strong supporter of the Italian monarchy, was named to succeed Mussolini.

In Palermo, where SI established its first major base, Mussolini's overthrow brought out huge crowds to celebrate. Church bells pealed throughout Italy. One of the most important benefits of the OSS's role in this invasion was the credibility that the organization gained with the staff of the Seventh Army and various combat divisions. The OSS was starting to earn the stripes that would be valuable in future operations.[3]

The capture of Sicily and the formation of a new government opened the way for negotiation of an Italian surrender. While negotiations with the Badoglio government were being conducted, final maneuvers were under way for the Salerno landing, Operation Avalanche. As part of the surrender deal, the Allies hoped to orchestrate anti-Fascist elements of the Italian Army to take over the airfields around Rome. Such a coup would have been a devastating setback for the Wehrmacht, but it never came off. It had been so hastily conceived that there was no chance to win support among the demoralized and underequipped Italian troops.

The Badoglio government begged for a delay in broadcasting the armistice terms, fearing that such an announcement would immediately lead the Germans to occupy Rome, hitherto a protected zone under Wehrmacht edict. This would have been the death knell of the new Badoglio government. General Eisenhower, learning that the airports around Rome could not be secured, refused Badoglio's request and announced the armistice on 8 September. At the same time, German forces began encircling Rome.

Hasty discussions ensued among the Badoglio entourage, the king, and the royal family, which had been holding on to a tenuous position in Rome. With no other options, the beleaguered royals adopted a last-ditch exit plan. In the dead of night, a convoy of five cars left the eastern gates of Rome, surreptitiously heading for the Adriatic port of Pescara. Here they kept a rendezvous with two Italian corvettes. By the morning of 10 September 1943, the royal family and minimal services of the anti-Fascist Italian government were installed in the Allied occupied city of Brindisi. This rump government, operating under the eyes of the Allied Commission, had no effective authority beyond the limits of its own compound.[4]

Meanwhile, the invasion of Salerno had begun. In the three months following the Sicily invasion, OSS Italy had augmented its capabilities in order to play a larger and more effective role in the first invasion of the Italian mainland. Fifth Army troopships approaching the Salerno beaches carried an OSS contingent. Donald Downes, OSS representative with G-2 Fifth Army, had arranged for forty agents to accompany the invading troops on condition that this group would assist the Army's Counter Intelligence Corps and other military security units. Shortly after the landing, small detachments were set up to provide combat intelligence to frontline troops through use of agents recruited on the spot.

Other agents were infiltrated through the lines for distances of ten to fifty miles. Another group of agents from the OSS base that was established in Palermo supported the Seventh Army troops.

Because Marshal Badoglio had failed to instruct his troops to turn against the Wehrmacht at Salerno, Gen. Mark Clark's Allied troops encountered heavy German opposition as they landed. Three days of bitter fighting followed, but the Germans could not force the Allies back into the sea. The German commander, Marshal Kesselring, realizing he could not hold his line of defense, began a retreat, while the British Eighth and the American Fifth Armies drove back the enemy's rearguards around Vesuvius and Pompei. On 1 October, they entered Naples. A major victory had been won, but most of Italy remained under German control.[5]

In October, the Allied 15th Army Group consisted of eleven divisions. It comprised the British Eighth Army, operating on the east, and the American Fifth on the west side of the peninsula. Despite the large size of these formations, the Allied advance up the peninsula continued to encounter stiff resistance. Marshal Kesselring took maximum advantage of every geographical feature to stall the Allied offensive. A prolonged stalemate at Monte Casino prompted Churchill to devise a closely held secret plan for an amphibious landing at Anzio, only thirty miles south of Rome. The Fifth Army units assigned to the attack were joined by a small OSS detachment that landed on 22 January 1944. The attackers succeeded in taking the enemy completely by surprise, and there were few German forces defending Rome on this southern flank. But a combination of Kesselring's brilliant defensive measures and timidity on the part of the American in command of the landing allowed the Germans to close their lines and delay the taking of Rome for five gory months, until 4 June.

With the liberation of Rome, the Allies recognized the Committee of National Liberation (CLN) as the provisional government of postwar Italy. Composed of a broad spectrum of political parties and anti-Fascist factions, it had been evolving since the early days of the German occupation. Until the liberation, a clandestine board of directors in Rome had governed its operations. It had its own internal divisions, notably a strong disagreement between pro- and anti-monarchists and a parallel division between Communist and anti-Communist groups. As an underground group supporting sabotage and terrorism against the Germans, the CLN embraced seemingly unbridgeable gaps within its membership.

So politicized and divided by intense factional rivalries was the CLN that it took six months of secret negotiations before their leaders and the top commands of American and British forces could reach an accord. That agreement, signed in Rome on 8 December 1944, provided for Allied financial aid as well as arms and supplies to the partisans, who until then had been receiving such assistance spasmodically and in smaller volumes than they needed.

An incipient resistance movement had developed at the time of Italy's surrender in September 1943, when growing numbers of Italian troops were deserting and coming together in clandestine bands to fight against the Germans. Over the next nine months, until the fall of Rome, the movement gained strength and coherence despite a Wehrmacht dragnet that executed fugitives from the military, after using the cruelest forms of torture. Just as the French Maquis had worked with sympathetic civilians to sabotage enemy occupiers, so the Italian partisan forces teamed with like-minded elements of local communities. Even so, it was a terrible era, tantamount to civil war, marked by bitter and bloody disputes between those who supported and those who opposed the partisan anti-Fascist activities.

Adding to the political turmoil of this period was the remarkable German operation that snatched Mussolini from his captors. In late August, Badoglio had transferred il Duce to a small mountain resort high in the Abruzzi of central Italy. On 12 September 1943, a troop of ninety German parachutists succeeded in a daring mission to liberate Mussolini and fly him off to a meeting with Hitler. The two dictators agreed on a scheme for reinstating the Italian Fascist regime, initially on the shores of Lake Como and subsequently at Lake Garda. Tightly reigned in by the Germans, this was never more than a shadow government, but nevertheless it represented a rival to the Badoglio administration in the south.

With the fall of Rome in 1944, the resistance movement gathered strength throughout the peninsula, with its stronghold in the industrial north. Here the Communist Party had found its greatest numbers of adherents and, consequently, its strongest influence. There are no solid data on which to base estimates of Communist membership in the resistance, but George Botjer, author of *The Sideshow War*, cites a figure of 40 percent.[6] The politics of the CLN in its Milan base, whether reflecting a Moscow-directed line or a more moderated version of it, were fiercely anti-monarchy, pro-labor, pro-republican, and staunchly socialist.

On 16 June 1944, twelve days after the fall of Rome, Ivanoe Bonomi, a seventy-three-year-old political independent, announced the formation of the *Comitato di Liberazione Nazionale per l'Alta Italia*, the CLNAI, a new government in which he would serve as premier. Marshal Badoglio was offered a cabinet post but refused. Italy's postwar government and the future of the monarchy were left for the electorate to determine after the war.

The only Italian general who ordered his division to fight the Germans during the Allied assault on Rome was Raffaele Cadorna who, as a third-generation professional soldier, was politically independent. Having turned against the Fascists, Cadorna lived for many months underground in the Eternal City as a hunted man. The CLNAI leadership, hoping to strengthen their connection to the Allies, decided to place Cadorna in the key position of military chief behind the lines. In August 1944, after receiving minimal parachute training under British Special

Operations Executive (SOE) auspices, he departed from an airstrip outside Rome to be dropped, along with a British team, near what would become his secret headquarters outside Milan. His mission involved exceptional risk because the Germans had learned to set off decoy flares in order to confuse Allied pilots. However, this deception tactic failed that night, and the general had a safe landing, enabling him to take up his critically important mission. Cadorna commanded great respect from the disparate elements represented in the CLN, and he played a vital role in mediating the many turf battles and political disputes that erupted between them.

On 21 September 1944, three months after the liberation of Rome, when the Allies had pushed north of Siena to what became known as the Gothic Line, I received orders to proceed from Algiers to OSS Caserta.[7] Long before my arrival, the OSS and its British cousins in SOE had been organizing Italian resistance into an increasingly effective "fourth arm" of the drive up the peninsula. Having been totally absorbed in my duties supporting the OGs in France, I'd been able to give only slight attention to Italy and knew nothing about the high-level debates on military strategy among the Allied leadership. I knew only that I would be serving with Special Operations, helping resistance forces behind enemy lines. I was thankful that but for the OSS, I could easily have been in one of the Army Field Artillery units fighting its way up the rugged Italian terrain.

Much to my surprise, I found that I would be working in a palace, albeit one with few remnants of its grander past. San Leucio was one of the original palaces of the kings of the two Sicilies, later to be the kings of Naples. Built on the top of a hill overlooking Naples, the old complex consisted of a main quadrangle surrounding a courtyard and various outbuildings. Before the OSS took it over, it had been converted into a silk mill, and bolts of the fabric remained in some unused parts of an annex. I recall going through this area with Maj. James Thompson, who later went on to develop the famous Thai silk business in Bangkok. Apparently knowing a good deal about the material even then, Jimmy helped me select a sample to take home after the war. Thompson was only one of the many interesting and colorful figures who were stationed at headquarters or else passing through en route to an operational mission.

As in the OSS headquarters in Algiers, all branches of the agency were represented in OSS Caserta, making for a sizable organization that included both military and civilian personnel. Not all of the staff could be housed in the main complex, so the women lived in rooms scattered around town. Enlisted personnel lived in a tent camp, and junior officers such as myself were billeted in an officers' barracks.

The road to San Leucio climbed a long, sloping hill adorned with Versailles-like fountains and statuary, part of the extensive gardens surrounding the grandeur with which Italian monarchs tried to emulate Louis XIV.

Statuary group, Caserta

The Caserta knockoff of Versailles, though large and imposing, fell short of the refinement and majesty achieved under the Sun King. But its scale was appropriate for the Allied Forces Headquarters, which filled all the gilded chambers and long, mirrored halls with offices of military commands. The somewhat shabby and much smaller OSS compound was conveniently near AFHQ; a shuttle bus and dedicated phone lines ensured communications.

On my arrival at the Caserta office, I reported at once to Col. William P. Davis, under whom I had served in Algiers. Davis's official title was now operations and training officer, and in that capacity he was responsible for SO, the Maritime Unit, Schools and Training, and Operational Supply. As he had in Algiers, he reported to G-3 for Operations at AFHQ. In short order, Davis told me I was being assigned as escort officer for the Papaya Mission.[8] This twenty-one-member group consisted of ten American military personnel, two American civilians of Italian extraction, and nine Italian partisans. They were to go first to a base on the French side of the Italian border, and, after crossing into Italy, conduct a series of sabotage operations against the German occupation. It was intended that ultimately, they would help to establish postliberation civil order.

Early in September, high-level OSS brass meeting in Caserta had agreed on objectives and tactics of the mission. The group would be divided into four teams, Papaya 1, 2, 3, and 4. They would establish a temporary base near Annecy and make contact with Renato Vanzetti, the assistant leader of SI Orange mission and a top partisan figure in the Val Pelice, a valley on the Italian side of the border.

My assignment was to escort the two U.S. Air Corps C-47s carrying this team, along with their seventy-five-pound baggage packs. I would pick them up in Siena and stay with them until Annecy. My main responsibility was to ensure that the group leader, Maj. John Tozzi, met the OSS representative in Annecy, Capt. Arturo Mathieu. He would lead them to the prearranged crossing spot on the border. On the Italian side, Orange would make contact and take them to a secured location.

Papaya seems to have been star-crossed from the outset. On the first leg of my trip, while flying aboard one of the C-47s to Siena, I discovered that due to confusion in supply channels, they had been issued no cold-weather gear even though winter was approaching. All I could do was to make certain the problem was corrected once we arrived in France—a task proving more difficult than anticipated.

Worse yet, I found upon our landing in Annecy that Papaya's arrival was completely unexpected. "No one there knew anything at all of the mission," I later wrote in my report.[9] Captain Mathieu had not, therefore, ordered the transport to take the group to the border. We had plenty to sort out! One of the team leaders, Capt. Joseph Bonfiglio, went off to the supply depot in Lyon in search of winter clothing and rations. Once there, he learned that the depot had been moved two hundred miles away. By the time Bonfiglio returned, Major Tozzi, four guides, and three other Papaya 2 members had already left to enter Val Pelice. Confusing radio-traffic signals had led Tozzi to the mistaken conclusion that Renato had authorized his departure.

I had left Annecy on the morning of 30 September, before Tozzi's premature departure. My plane had a schedule to keep, and I considered my duty accomplished once Tozzi and Mathieu had met. They assured me they had conferred on the mission, and were sure that the transport for moving Papaya to the border would be available within a few days. Captain Mathieu gave his assurance that he would keep Caserta and Siena posted on the mission's progress.

The plane's next destination was Paris, where I spent the better part of two days reveling in the magical atmosphere of the liberation, won only one month earlier. I remember walking among exuberant crowds on the Champs-Elysées and bumping into a Princeton classmate, my friend Sandy Lewis. Back in Caserta on 3 October, I submitted my mission report to Colonel Davis.

Before long we learned of Papaya's fate. Major Tozzi, having misread signals and led his eight-man group across the border on his own initiative, was unprepared for the situation they encountered. The Germans soon spotted the team, who in a dense fog ended up less than five hundred meters from an enemy artillery battery. There was a desperate gunfight in which the team ran out of ammunition and was forced to surrender. All wore military uniforms, yet a German military tribunal initially charged them with espionage. Fortunately, they wound up in a POW camp where, for some reason, they were not interrogated closely and thus were saved from torture or possible execution. One guide, named Gayot, managed to escape with a captured German cipher book. Papaya teams 1 and 3, under Bonfiglio's command, remained on the French side and helped to organize the overland supply route to Italian partisans and clear the area of German troops.

Papaya 4 was to be infiltrated into Piedmont to join up with one of the Communist partisan groups. Originally, it was to be headed by Lt. Irving Goff, one of the twenty members of the Lincoln Brigade of the Spanish Civil War who had joined the OSS along with Donald Downes. Because Goff was involved in another mission, the group was taken over by another Lincoln Brigade graduate, Lt. Milton Wolf. When this group decided to forego their military uniforms and cross the border into Italy as civilians, Lieutenant Wolf proceeded on to the OSS base in Grenoble.[10]

The OSS unit in Annemasse, later to be designated Detachment F, was under the command of Col. Kenneth Baker, with whom I had served on the SPOC staff in Algiers. Its main mission became supplying the Italian partisans with arms, ammunition, clothing, and sabotage materials, plus intelligence on enemy locations. Two SO agents, Lt. Michael A. Jiminez, who also had been in the Lincoln Brigade, and Irving Singer, arranged for partisan porters to take supplies "by manback" across the rugged terrain. This method of transport was necessary because poor weather conditions resulted in the failure of two out of three supply drops. Thirty-five tons of supplies were delivered by manback.[11]

Papaya's mission, like that of Detachment F, was complicated from the outset by opposition from French groups seeking to annex the Italian regions across the border, notably the Val d'Aosta. These groups enjoyed full support and encouragement from General de Gaulle. They resented any interference that might jeopardize their geopolitical aims, especially a mission organized by American intelligence services. Nevertheless, the principal cause of Papaya 2's failure remains Major Tozzi's misreading of signals. The ensuing capture and internment of all but the one guide who escaped hardly represented an auspicious beginning for the new phase of "my war."

On my way back from France, I became tangentially involved in a complicated organizational controversy, involving top levels of Allied military commands far beyond the limited sphere of my experience. My plane from Paris was directed to stop over in Lyon, where I was instructed to report to SFU4, the forward arm of SPOC that represented OSS Algiers with the Seventh Army. There I found myself attending a conference with the unit's American commanding officer, Colonel Bartlett. When I reread my report on this conference today, I wonder first how anyone of my junior rank could have been sitting in such a high-level meeting, and second how, in the fog of war, the differing agendas of the OSS and the military commands to whom we reported could have been reconciled.

The future of SFU4, which had played a vital role in the invasion of southern France, now seemed to depend on results of a conference to be held in Versailles. Colonel Bartlett did not even know whether SFU4 currently reported to SHAEF in London or to AFHQ in Caserta. Whether SFU4 would have a role in the entry of Allied forces into Germany was being hotly debated. Considerable friction and what seemed like bureaucratic rivalry had developed between SFU4 and the Sixth Army's Special Operations unit, which was bypassing SFU4 in laying on operations behind enemy lines. A Sixth Army headquarters colonel, reputedly always making trouble for OSS, had proposed sending OG teams behind the lines in Germany. But Colonel Bartlett would not acquiesce in this plan, since SFU4 was not allowed to enter Sixth Army's war room to find out where the front lines ran.[12]

With only the sketchiest understanding of the issues involved, I nevertheless prepared the report on these meetings for my superiors in headquarters. Back in Caserta, I tried to figure out my future role in this confusing organizational environment. All these years later, in searching through the archives, I have been able to confirm the extent of disarray in the Special Operations branch at this time. In a 24 September 1944 "theater officer pouch review" from Washington, a report on Special Operations Caserta reads: "There is *no* head, *no* SO organization, *no* one to report SO activities. Top officers agree that SO has been despoiled by other branches . . . speed of events did not permit preservation of SO as an entity."[13]

The SO branch was not the only weak spot in Caserta's organization. It appears in hindsight that there were many other problem areas in the headquarters structure. The OSS regimental commander with the title strategic services officer was Col. Edwin J. F. Glavin, a graduate of West Point and Oxford. Gossip among OSS insiders held that Donovan valued Glavin's political connections in the Republican Party—specifically in the camp of Governor Dewey—as a means of ensuring the postwar future of the OSS.[14] It was also rumored, though, that Donovan had quite a low regard for Glavin. Moreover, insiders recognized that Glavin's executive officer, Col. Thomas Early, had received his appointment because of his family connections to President Roosevelt, which might help to safeguard the OSS should the presidential election go the other way. Both Glavin and Early have since received some negative criticism as administrators. For example, in his 1972 history of the OSS, Harris Smith summed up the situation at Caserta headquarters as follows: "The Theater staff was held together through the ability of Glavin's adjutant, Norman Newhouse, the son of immigrant Russian Jews and editor of a Long Island newspaper."[15]

In Glavin's defense, it should be noted that he inherited something of a mixed bag when he took command of the regiment in Caserta. Before he came on the scene, constant changes in the officers named to head OSS Italy had damaged credibility with the military, while creating confusion and unease within the staff. To provide for a more integrated and responsive organizational structure, Glavin made the decision to merge all OSS activities and units under a single command.

Donovan's intuitive understanding of command and control led him to compensate for weaknesses at the top by placing able individuals in charge of operational branches. For instance, Colonel Davis, who had accomplished so much in the complex political environment of Algiers, continued to head the Operations Section in Caserta. And William P. Maddox, a Princeton academic and political scientist who had served in the SI Branch in London, became chief of SI MEDTO in Caserta. His deputy was the distinguished Harvard law professor Milton Katz. The chief financial officer, another Harvard product, was David Crockett, a wizard in the vagaries of Europe's wartime currencies both official and black-market. Kermit Roosevelt, also a Harvard alumnus, was beginning to prepare for his postwar position as chief historian of the OSS. John Gardner of Mount Holyoke was on the OSS psychological staff involved in testing and selecting candidates for SO and SI missions.

The academic institutions and backgrounds that these officers represented were typical of Caserta senior staff. On the distaff side, women of comparable educational pedigrees worked in Research and Analysis, Registry, and the Message Center. The many shared academic and social origins of headquarters personnel along with the beauty of our physical surroundings and the excitement of our work made for a congenial and spirited social life, causing some of us to feel occasional twinges of guilt. But as I remember it, none of us ever lost sight of the critical importance of our work in support of winning a war. Reminders of that fact, if we needed them, were the frequent visitors who came through Caserta en route to the dangerous missions for which they had volunteered on all fronts.

Many of these individuals came from far less elite backgrounds. For example, Irving Goff, the most colorful, outgoing, and outspoken of the Lincoln Brigade graduates, was summoned to Caserta twice to be queried concerning the allegedly pro-Communist content of his orders to the partisans he controlled. Goff described himself as a kid from Brooklyn who had never seen a mountain until he was fighting in Spain.

Like many other operations personnel in the field, Goff held Caserta headquarters in the lowest regard. In one interview, he dismissed it with, "Never knew any of the stuff going on with the top officers."[16] In my several encounters with Goff, he was bright and engaging, with arguments in favor of supporting the Communist partisans that mostly made good sense. I also came to understand how such an action-oriented operator, often risking his life in daring missions behind enemy lines, would have little sympathy for deskbound bureaucrats. Antagonism between headquarters and field is often the cause of difficult organizational relationships, whether in military or civilian structures. The OSS in Italy had its full share of such problems.

Col. William Maddox, chief of SI for the entire Mediterranean Theater, inherited a particularly tough problem in having to deal with the large free-wheeling, sometimes contentious Italian SI section. Its operational headquarters had been established across the peninsula in the center of the city of Brindisi. After the fall of Rome, SI established a station there and moved SI's political, economic, and industrial intelligence sections from Caserta. Scamporino had led an SI team into Rome along with the Allied advance units, charged with searching buildings for documents and intelligence. By late August 1944, the Rome station had established a reports section to handle technical translations and political intelligence while maintaining unofficial contacts with the Vatican and high levels of the remaining Italian government. Scamporino was chief of the Rome station while Corvo headed SI operations.

Another top officer of the Rome station was Lt. Col. John Ricca, a native of Detroit, who had been chief prosecutor of the Detroit Municipal Court. The son of Italian immigrants from Piemonte, he grew up speaking the pure Piemontese dialect at home. Partly because this was the Italian that Marshal Badoglio spoke, the two men formed a close bond. Ricca handled liaison with *Servicio Italiano Militare* (SIM), the Italian intelligence agency, and helped to promote the movement of many SI agents into CLNAI's intelligence organization.

Although, as we have seen, SI worked closely and effectively with other branches on missions in the field, it earned a reputation at AFHQ and OSS Caserta as an unruly group of Italian Americans. Dubbed the Mafiosi, they were seen as running SI Italy as their own fiefdom. A spurious kind of logic was at play in this perception. Many Italians in north and central Italy looked down on Sicilians as an inferior, hot-blooded breed. Corvo and Scamporino were both of Sicilian descent, as were many of their recruits. Therefore, by this logic, all SI personnel were tarred with the brush of inferiority. In fact, the SI personnel complement consisted of individuals with family ties to many different parts of Italy, as in the case of John Ricca. Moreover, the Sicilian Americans and the partisans with whom they worked proved their worth beyond doubt, in successfully executing many important and dangerous missions.

Another specious claim about SI personnel was that they were all socialists. Many of the Italian-American Connecticut contingent came from union backgrounds, but few were actively associated with the Socialist Party. Scamporino had been a labor union attorney in Connecticut, but Corvo was a conservative Republican. However, it is generally acknowledged that Scamporino, or "Scamp," could be particularly combative in interpersonal relations. He tended to alienate some of his peers in other branches, as well as his superiors in the OSS hierarchy. But the two senior officers cared deeply about their own personnel in the field, whose lives were being risked. They felt that their operations deserved far greater recognition and support from headquarters.

SI Brindisi frequently complained to Caserta headquarters about lack of sufficient support personnel, inadequate supplies of equipment, and poor radio systems linking SI Rome, the Brindisi base, and the field. Emilio Daddario, serving as head of operations and training in Brindisi, was often called on to mediate disputes. Temperamentally well equipped to serve as moderator, Mim, as he was called, was Corvo's closest collaborator. As the officer in charge of parachute training who supervised each mission's departure for their drop zones in north Italy and monitored all the cable traffic, Daddario was the individual best informed about all the SI missions in the field.

Eight days after my return from France, I was sent to Siena for the first of several meetings with Capt. William Suhling, commanding officer of Company D of the 2677th Regiment. Formed in July 1944, Company D had moved from Rome to Siena.[17] Suhling reported directly to G-3 Special Operations, 15th Army Group, the unit responsible for coordinating all Allied Special Operations into enemy-occupied Italy.

Two forward detachments, one with the Fifth Army and a second with the Eighth Army, reported directly to Company D, as did the Maritime Unit operating on the Adriatic with Italian marines of the San Marco Battalion. The commander of MU was Lt. Robert Kelly, who was attached to the Eighth Army. The unit was made up of highly skilled, well-disciplined, and courageous Italian sailors eager to fight the Germans. They conducted a number of important missions involving the infiltration of San Marco commandos deep behind enemy lines to work with the partisans. One of the most daring and fruitful operations, codenamed Packard, consisted of a San Marco officer, two enlisted men, and a partisan engineer. They penetrated the Gothic Line defenses and brought out complete plans of those defenses, from the coast to thirty kilometers inland. This extremely valuable information actually permitted the Eighth Army to carry out a short-lived break through the defenses shortly thereafter.[18] The Fifth Army detachment, at its peak, consisted of about forty officers and enlisted men, together with some thirty on loan from the OG 2671st Special Reconnaissance Battalion. The Eighth Army detachment was smaller than the Fifth, consisting at its peak of four officers and fifteen enlisted men.

With the concentration of control of actual field operations in Company D, the function of the Operations office in Caserta where I served had become largely liaison. This visit was my initiation as a liaison officer between SO Caserta and the several operational detachments of our regiment. At this time, the Germans were buttressed behind the Gothic Line. This defensive barrier stretched from the west coast, twelve miles above Pisa, to Rimini on the east coast. The line was less than an hour's drive north of Siena. Its construction was mostly complete by late August 1944, when the Allies were debating the prospects for breaching it.[19]

The fortifications consisted of a network of bunkers, minefields, and tank traps to defend the great valley of the Po River. Hitler had originally planned to allow the Allies to advance up the boot while he held on only to northern Italy. But Kesselring persuaded him to reinforce the Gothic Line and hold it. Some of the top Allied commanders, following Churchill's strategy, advocated an assault before winter made the terrain impassable, but that option was deemed too costly. The power of the Allied forces had been sharply reduced by the transfer of American and British divisions to France. Being stalemated in this stage of the campaign, military commanders found the partisan resistance groups increasingly important, both as a source of intelligence on enemy troop deployment and also as instruments of harassment and sabotage.

Suhling's job was to ensure that the partisans were engaged to optimal effect in support of the military. At middle age, he had volunteered for the OSS from the Army Medical Administration Corps. A gentleman farmer from Frederick, Virginia, Suhling had a pleasant demeanor and agreeable Southern drawl. More important, he had more than enough horse sense to make up for his total lack of intelligence background.[20]

Suhling faced many challenges, including dealing with partisan groups drawn from a broad political spectrum. The Italian resistance was a political stew representing Communist, socialist, Christian Democrat, republican, and monarchist parties as well as the Action Party, a leftist coalition. Each group was competing for arms, food, and other supplies, as well as assignment of missions with promise for recognition and reward. This confusion would not be even partially resolved until the consolidation under the CLNAI, in June 1944. Meanwhile, Suhling and all other OSS decision-makers faced difficult choices in relation to partisan resistance. The Communist groups, usually the most aggressive, could be counted on for more daring missions, but our British counterparts consistently warned of the risks in supplying them with weapons they could use to pursue political aims after the war.

Another difficult relationship for Suhling and Company D involved ties with the British SOE and its No. 1 Special Force, particularly in the competition for air transportation. Until January 1945, the British Air Operations Section in Brindisi packed all OSS supplies, most of which had been reverse lend-leased to the United States. An acute shortage of U.S. planes and pilots hampered all efforts to drop OSS teams behind enemy lines and to keep them supplied. AFHQ and 15th Army Group allocations of aircraft to the OSS always fell short of the need presented by new SO, OG, and SI teams arriving in the field. Because of this shortage of equipment, the Americans had to plead with the British for transport, but the British, not surprisingly, tended to favor their own operations.

Shortage of trained air operations personnel was a serious limitation. The British were sufficiently staffed to maintain an officer with each squadron for briefing and debriefing crews, as well as a chief air liaison officer for each group of squadrons. The United States had too few qualified officers to match this procedure. The Americans were in a catch-22 bind, since apportionment of tonnage to operating agencies was based on the number of tons allocated in previous months. Because the OSS had not been able to obtain the necessary airlift to support its missions in the past, it accumulated a large backlog of unfilled supply requests.

Moreover, nearly the entire Royal Air Force 334 Wing, which had been servicing both SOE and OSS out of Brindisi, was destroyed in missions over Warsaw. Those efforts resulted in a tragic loss of airmen and planes, and all in vain because the Wermacht mercilessly stamped down the heroic uprising of the Polish resistance. Ultimately, it was necessary for General Donovan to intervene at the highest level to obtain a U.S. Air Force agreement to carry on the job of OSS resupply in Italy. Patch's Seventh Army advance in southern France hastened availability of the U.S. planes.[21]

Suhling quickly recognized the difficulty of conducting OSS air operations in northern Italy from the Brindisi air base, on the Italian heel. The difference in weather patterns between Brindisi and the drop zones always presented problems in mounting operations. Suhling's arguments were a major factor in persuading the 15th Army Group to move the base north, first to Malignano airfield, near Siena, and later to Rosignano.

The lines of command for Company D could hardly have been more complicated. On the OSS side, Suhling reported to Col. Edwin J. F. Glavin, CO of the 2677 Regiment in Caserta. Glavin's early decision to bring each of OSS's five operational branches into the regiment created a complex chain of command. Competition for resources and personality clashes among the branches were not uncommon. On the military side, Suhling reported to G-3 15th Army Group, where he often encountered antagonism to OSS intelligence operations. Keeping all these lines of communication in order was a challenge calling for the exceptional skills that Suhling brought to his job. Each of my later meetings with him reinforced my high regard for his capability.

Serving as chief of Special Operations in Company D and as Suhling's right-hand man was Maj. Judson B. Smith, who came to be my principal point of contact. Smith had inherited certain prejudices from his Southern background, and he was not very tolerant of some of the Italo-Americans in the SI branch. Relations between Smith and SI's top leaders were often strained.

Another surprise awaited me on returning to Caserta. After I reported to Bill Davis the results of my Siena meetings, he told me that he was sending me to Capri for some R and R. Although I felt no need for R and R, Davis had already issued travel orders, and the chance of visiting this fabled island was too tempting to resist. Also I had heard glowing accounts of the OSS villa there.

The initial OSS presence on Capri came about at the time of the Salerno invasion, on 19 September 1943. The OSS had been assigned a special task to look after the safety of the famous philosopher Benedetto Croce, who had a home on Capri. He was one of the few prominent intellectuals allowed to criticize the Fascist regime openly, and the Allies realized that Italians would take great offense at any mishap to his person.[22] When Croce was trapped behind enemy lines in the advance on Naples, a British SOE team rescued him. Later Donovan became involved in a plot that Croce conceived to form a left-wing Italian legion to act as a rallying point against the Germans. Donovan's endorsement of this plan may have seemed incompatible with his customary commitment to the British in supporting the Italian monarchy. In fact, however, Donovan's pragmatism allowed him to side with whatever political faction seemed most likely to advance the cause of the Allied military campaign.

During the Salerno campaign, Capri became an important OSS communications base as well as a center for planning and launching maritime operations. The Allied patrol boat fleet was moored there. Clandestine sea transportation was often preferable to the dangerous line-crossing operations on land. Donovan used Capri often as his command post to direct both the land and sea operations in support of the military assault on Naples. OSS personnel on Capri interviewed the many Neapolitans who fled to Capri and Ischia during the attack, and they recruited dozens of agents for short-term intelligence missions. OSS agents, using the Capri link, transmitted the first intelligence on the disintegration of the Italian army forces after Salerno, and on the battles between Italian and German forces south of Rome.

The OSS had been offered the use of Villa Fortini, which belonged to the prominent New York socialite Mona Williams. She was married to Harrison Williams, a wealthy businessman who had made one of the largest contributions to General Donovan's 1932 New York gubernatorial campaign. During the war, the property was intended for use as both a location for OSS conclaves and also as an R and R refuge for agency personnel. In return for this generous loan, the OSS was expected to safeguard the property and all its historic treasures. The villa was on the site of several structures attributed to Emperor Tiberius, on a high bluff overlooking the sea. Well-preserved mosaics, frescoes, and sculptures were everywhere. The Williamses, naturally, wanted these treasures protected and believed that the people Donovan recruited would be good temporary custodians. Indeed, Donovan had persuaded Mrs. Williams that her villa would be in better hands with the OSS than if it were taken over by regular military troops.

The villa proved to be a serious bone of contention within the agency. Donovan first asked Donald Downes, who had served so bravely and effectively at Salerno, to take command of the site. He had been one of the twelve American vice-consuls in Vichy-controlled North Africa, from where he subsequently conducted intelligence operations into Spain. Serving directly under Donovan at Salerno, Downes had displayed great courage and determination behind enemy lines. His staunch idealism was coupled with a keen ambition, and he eagerly sought a top position in the OSS. But when offered command of the Capri post in the Williams villa, he rejected it with the words, "I don't want to fight a war protecting Mrs. Williams's pleasure dome."[23] In a stormy meeting that night with Donovan, Downes was dismissed and his career was temporarily sidelined.

According to the considerable literature on that career, Downes was one of the most colorful and controversial officers in the OSS. One 1987 book on major academics within the OSS maintains that no other OSS figure was so nearly "the complete spy."[24] Downes ran Operation Banana out of North Africa into Spain, said to have been one of the worst intelligence disasters in the era of the Spanish Civil War. On joining the OSS with Donovan's encouragement and assistance, he brought along a group of twenty hand-picked American leftists and Spaniards who had served in the Lincoln Brigade. The Americans were among the few who could claim combat experience in partisan warfare. Further substantiating the view that he was the consummate spy is the allegation that he also spied for British intelligence.[25]

At the start of the Italian campaign, Downes had been contending for advancement with Ellery Huntington, a rich Wall Street lawyer and product of Yale, a perfect example of the type that Donovan so admired. Huntington not only had the correct social background, he also displayed remarkable courage and was always willing to put himself at risk. He possessed the same kind of bravery that Donovan had exhibited in World War I and in early OSS missions. It was not surprising, therefore, that he was given command of all the OSS assets in the Salerno area. Eventually, he assumed command of all OSS operations in Yugoslavia.

In October 1944, a year after the Salerno invasion, the assault on Naples, and the establishment of the OSS base on Capri, I boarded a launch in Naples, bound for my R and R in Mrs. Williams's incredibly beautiful villa. The front lines of the war had moved almost three hundred miles up the Italian peninsula. Capri was reverting to its characteristic *dolce vita*. And here I was, along with a group of six or so other OSS men and women, sent off for what amounted to a weekend house party. Without even wondering what I had done to deserve all this, I set about enjoying all that Capri had to offer—which was a great deal indeed.

Villa Fortini consisted of several separate buildings constructed over the ruins of a Tiberian site. Thus, the master bedroom suite, guest quarters, and dining room were each in separate units, set apart in lovely landscaped grounds.

Oddly, one thing I remember quite clearly is one of the women in our party taking me to see the closets and armoires that held Mona's huge wardrobe. She evidently had a passion for suede, judging by the quantity of such creations in one particular armoire.

We spent our days under the warm October sun, exploring the island on foot. We walked down to the main harbor, picturesque even though still used as a base for Allied naval vessels, climbed up to Ana Capri and Axel Munthe's Villa San Michele, and visited the famous Blue Grotto, on a local boatman's craft. Picnics and *al fresco* lunches in small restaurants were followed, at day's end, by cocktails and dinner at our villa. Each day was a perfect idyll. When it was time to leave, we were informed that the seas were too rough for the OSS launch. We would have to spend an extra day on the island before returning to Caserta. We received this news with stoic courage.

Back at the office, I found we were busily engaged in responding to a request from the CLNAI. The account of that activity follows, as reported in the Company D "History of the Operations Section."[26]

In October, the OSS had been asked to send American personnel into northern Italy for liaison with the partisan zonal commands in order to tie the partisan effort more closely to Allied strategy. U.S. Army personnel formed into OSS teams for this purpose received intensive training and were dispatched to the field. Shortly before departure, each team received a thorough briefing on the CLNAI and the partisan movement, and on the military, political, and economic situation in the area to which the team was going. Additionally, they reviewed the 15th Army Group directive listing their duties. The Air Corps instructed the teams in the proper method of requesting bombings and reporting bomb damage. A representative of G-3 Special Operations 15th Army Group specified the role that each team was to play in the overall Allied strategy.

Teams ready for the field were taken to an area near the airport and equipped with parachutes and "striptease," or jumpsuits. A conducting officer saw the teams aboard and often went on the flight, to make sure that conditions at the pinpoint were favorable. All teams were dropped at night. Relatively few jumped blind; in most cases, agents already in the field selected pinpoints and arranged for reception by groups of partisans. Often unfavorable weather, lack of proper reception, faulty navigation, or engine trouble caused the planes to turn back, and some teams flew over their target area many times before being successfully dropped.

A radio operator went along with each team but, because of the high percentage of sets broken in dropping, some teams were unable to contact the base. Eventually, reserve sets were sent with each team. Through radio contact with agents the Operations Section directed their movements and activities, designated specific objectives, and transmitted orders from the 15th Army Group.

Radio bases for agent circuits were also established at the Fifth and Eighth Army detachments to ensure prompt reception of tactical intelligence transmitted by teams close behind the enemy lines.

In late November, I was assigned to another liaison mission with OSS posts in Bari and Brindisi. The port city of Brindisi had become an important Allied base soon after Mussonlini's arrest and the establishment of the new government, in fall 1943. Marshal Pietro Badoglio's government moved its base here after the fall of Rome. The Allied Control Commission, on which Gen. Maxwell Taylor served as U.S. representative, also settled here. Concurrently, the SI branch of the OSS selected Brindisi as its principal strategic infiltration base. Brindisi was uniquely situated as a logistical hub overlooking the Adriatic and the Balkans and as a post for overseeing the campaign up the boot of Italy.

I was one of three men on this mission, which was headed by Maj. Walter Ross, CO of Company B, the OSS Bari station. Lt. George Vujnovich of the Yugoslav desk was also on board our plane. Our assignment was to meet with OSS staff officers of the Air Resupply Detachment (ARSD) to assess the prospects for completing certain air operations then scheduled. The ARSD supervised the packing of supplies for OSS teams and equipped agents for parachute jumps. With the loss of the RAF 334 Wing (noted above), the shortage of air transportation had become the major problem for OSS operations in northern Italy, the Balkans, Austria, and Hungary, hampering all efforts to support resistance movements in German-occupied territory.

In our meeting with squadron leader Brown, it became clear that prospects for air support of the Italian Special Operations missions were not favorable, mainly because of weather. Late fall and winter weather, together with the need for sufficient moonlight at drop zones, limited the flight possibilities to as little as one night per month.

There were always more requests for air support than ARSD could handle, and AFHQ assigned priorities according to strategic considerations. Good weather for flying to distant pinpoints in the north swelled the demand for aircraft, and at such times all available planes were in operation. As a general rule, there were more operations on the board than could be flown. Due to an increase in heavy flak from antiaircraft guns, safe flight routes were limited. Squadron leader Brown advised us that only missions of highest urgency and extreme importance would be flown. I returned from this meeting with a fuller understanding of the problems confronting those charged with air transportation, as well as the conviction that henceforth it would be essential for Special Operations Caserta to maintain the closest communication with leaders of the ARSD.[27]

Back in headquarters after my Brindisi visit, I was to learn more about the complexities of the resistance movement. The Italian propensity for political infighting had prevented the various elements of the resistance from joining in a unified organization since the beginning of the war. A fierce struggle was being waged among a wide range of anti-Fascist resistance forces. The spectrum of political affiliations presented a bewildering array. Six main political parties were in a constant state of flux, with offshoots and mergers that only a few outsiders could fully comprehend. For the Allied commands seeking to support resistance movements, the chaos undermined trust of the partisans and nurtured doubts about ever achieving consolidation.

The SOE and British military commands tended to favor pro-monarchy groups, as we have seen, while the OSS took its cue from General Donovan's pragmatic position to support whichever groups would carry out their assigned mission most effectively, regardless of political connections.

By the third week of November, the OSS and SOE had succeeded in clearing the way for a delegation of three top CLNAI leaders to travel south from Milan to Rome via an underground route through Switzerland and France. As noted in a 20 November cable, the three delegates were Parri, Longhi, and Mare. The cable states, "Longhi is President of CLNAI, Parri is Deputy Commander NIPC, and Mare is Communist Representative in CLNAI Military Council." The delegation was seeking to obtain official Allied recognition of CLNAI as "an integral part of the present Italian government," and the Bonomi government was "in full accord." Finally, "the unity of all political parties in North Italy is such that CLNAI can guarantee complete order after withdrawal of Germans."[28]

Just as negotiations were about to start, the OSS discovered that British SOE, "our friends" whom we sometimes called "our cousins," were trying to reach a deal with the Italians behind our backs that would have left us on the sidelines. In a 25 November cable, Norman Newhouse, the able executive officer of OSS headquarters, reported to Colonel Glavin: "SOE has been negotiating with CLN to exclusion of our interest and investment both in personnel and finance." Despite such tricky maneuvering, the cable elaborated, CLN "has been unfavorably impressed with British attempts to count us out by jumping the gun on our talks." Having discovered the British ploy, the OSS was able to resume its place in the negotiations—but the incident does underscore how even our "friends" were sowing landmines on our path.[29]

By December 1944, the six political parties finalized an agreement to consolidate in the CLNAI. The accord was formalized in the Rome Protocols, recognizing the CLNAI as a virtual extension of the Bonomi government in northern Italy and declaring its commitment to democratic principles. Specifically citing its abhorrence of *reazione,* the accord thereby proclaimed its opposition to the monarchy. With the signing of the Protocols, the Allies undertook to support the CLNAI by contributing 180 million lire per month.

The military counterpart of the Protocols was the Caserta Agreement, signed at Fifth Army headquarters and committing the Allies to supply the partisan bands. It effectively placed the CLNAI and the resistance movement under the direct control of Allied military commands. The agreement stipulated that once the war was over, the partisans would turn in their weapons at Allied check-points. This provision was intended to remove the fangs from radical elements on the domestic political scene.

Serving on the Special Operations staff under Colonel Davis, I spent much of my time representing the SO at meetings at AFHQ where I, as a newcomer, was dealing with much higher-ranking colleagues who had been working together for many months. The issues before us centered on how to take fullest advantage of the partisans' capabilities to disrupt the Germans. In practical terms we had to decide on a daily basis how to allocate air transportation and supplies among all the groups clamoring for support.

Much of the debate revolved around the pros and cons of supporting par-tisan groups controlled by Communists. The British attitude was colored by their experience in Greece. From the outset of the war the British had been contend-ing with growth of the Communist movement in Greece and the threat it repre-sented to Britain's longstanding position of influence there. Substantial numbers of British troops were stationed there to ensure the return of Greece's King George II, exiled in Cairo. Churchill's insistent support of the monarchy became a major source of British-U.S. tension as the war progressed. The Roosevelt administra-tion, recognizing antipathy from segments of the American public, was firmly opposed to the British reliance on puppet regimes to maintain their empire.

These differences echoed throughout debates on support of the Italian par-tisans. The British argued in favor of cutting off or restricting supplies to the Garibaldini brigades, consisting mainly of Communist elements. However, as a rule these partisans were more aggressive and daring in their operations, and they inflicted more damage on the Axis forces than did other partisan groups. They fielded special "urban guerrilla units" known as Gappisti, or *Gruppi d'Azione Patriotica* (GAP), that took on particularly dangerous missions such as assassina-tions of Fascist officials or German officers. The Gappisti operated under the restraining wing of General Cadorna, who directed their energies into operations with the biggest payoff at well-calculated levels of risk.[30]

One of the most contentious issues in the affairs of OSS Italy began boiling up in the fall of 1944 with controversy over the activities of Lt. Irving Goff. Earlier that year, in the spring, Major Koch, then chief of Operations OSS Italy, had asked Goff to recruit some thirty to thirty-five agents from the Italian socialist and Communist parties in the belief that their prior experience in fighting Fascists would equip them to work with OSS-supported partisan groups. Koch promised that in return for their service, the agents could transmit Communist messages via OSS radio. It was agreed that such communications would be confined to partisan operations and that political propaganda would not be allowed. Copies of all traffic would be provided to Company D officers and maintained in their files.

Goff and three of his fellow officers, lieutenants Milton Wolff, Irving Fajans, and Vincent Lessowski, had served in the Lincoln Brigade in Spain and were alleged to be Communists or Communist sympathizers. Having been originally brought into the OSS under General Donovan's wing, Goff seemed to enjoy protection from opponents within the OSS. Scamporino, one of his chief antagonists, claimed that much of the Goff chain's cable traffic held hidden Communist messages. After several internal investigations, three of Goff's superiors, Maj. Judson Smith, Maj. William Suhling, and Lt. Col. William Maddox, all went on record in his defense. They argued first that it would be a breach of promise to go back on the original agreement that Koch had made with Goff, and second that the Goff chain's intelligence was of great value to 15th Army Group.[31]

After the war, Goff became chairman of the Communist Party in Louisiana and head of the Veterans Committee of the Communist Party of New York. When he was listed on the honor role of the Young Communist League, General Donovan came under fire for hiring Communists. His famous retort to this accusation was, "I don't know if he's on the Communist honor role, but for the job he did in Africa and Italy, he's on the honor role of OSS." Donovan always respected Goff, and the two men had a special relationship formed from their shared experiences in a number of daring missions. However, Goff and his chain became a major factor in the postwar decision against appointing Donovan as head of the OSS successor agency.

Global politics at the highest level came into play on the Italian battlefront. An understanding reached between Roosevelt, Churchill, and Stalin about postwar zones of influence in liberated Europe had an impact all the way down to levels of partisan resistance. Stalin agreed to concede Italy to the West in exchange for the Eastern European countries closer to the Soviet Union. Palmiro Togliatti, head of the Italian Communist Party, generally took his cue from Moscow but was an unpredictable figure, vacillating between the party line and a tack he deemed more likely to advance his cause with the broader Italian electorate after the war.[32] The OSS played an important role in dealing with Italian Communists toward the end of the war, as we shall see in chapter 5.

In mid-November, it became apparent that the Allied military goal of penetrating the Gothic Line could not be accomplished before spring. Recognizing that the terrain, the weather, and the relative strengths of the defending and attacking forces made continuing advances impossible, Gen. Harold Alexander of 15th Army Group broadcast a message to the resistance movement calling for a stand-down of their activities during winter months. He thanked them for their valuable help during the summer campaign but cautioned them about the difficulty of continuing resupply sorties and especially the risk of mounting any large-scale operations. He urged them to conserve ammunition and supplies. The partisans were instructed to leave their mountain hideouts and, whenever possible, return to their villages until they received instructions in the spring to resume operations.

This message was well intentioned but had a negative impact. Generally, the CLNAI and partisans misconstrued it as a veiled abandonment. In time, the misunderstanding was corrected by clarifying messages. What really restored partisans' hopes, however, was a sharp increase in tonnages dropped beginning in February 1945. Exceptionally good weather, at odds with all forecasts, allowed an increase from 181 tons in January to 591 in February.

One of the most notorious and troublesome mysteries of the OSS Italian experience remains the fate of Maj. William Hollohan, with whom I had served briefly on the SPOC staff in Algiers. So much has been written about this case that I will sketch only the highlights of the Hollohan story.

Then-Capt. William Hollohan was serving as executive officer in Company D, Siena, under Suhling, when General Donovan selected him as head of a very important mission to be dropped into an area about fifty miles north of Milan. Its principal objective was to serve as the official OSS liaison with the partisan resistance under the CLNAI in the period leading up to and after the defeat of the Germans. Nearly all phases of the OSS were incorporated, and the mission was actually a merger of two teams, Mangosteen (SI) and Chrysler (OG).

Initial concerns about the fact that Hollohan spoke no Italian were partially allayed by the belief that an American without ties to any Italian party would be perceived as above the influence of internal resistance politics. Hollohan was given a temporary promotion to the field officer rank of major. Aldo Icardi, a twenty-three-year-old Italian American, was appointed head of the SI section of the mission. The team was dropped to its reception committee successfully on 26 September. Hollohan and Icardi met immediately with Ferrucio Parri, Action Party leader and co-chairman of the CLN, who warmly welcomed the Americans. Hollohan was carrying sixteen thousand dollars in operational funds.

Because of the stand-down in resistance activity and the cutback in supplies of clothing and ammunition, each of the few planeloads dropped became increasingly vital to the survival of the partisan groups. They were suffering severely from enemy assaults and the harsh winter weather. The difficult task of arbitrating among the groups contending for these supplies fell on Hollohan's team. One Moscow-trained leader of a Communist-oriented group was particularly outraged when forty-four automatic weapons that he expected were dropped to a group of Christian Democrats that he considered far less capable of using the weapons.

In December the villa where the team was quartered came under attack and all members scattered. Later, when it was safe to reassemble at another prearranged site, Hollohan never reappeared. At first it was feared he might have been captured, but no overtures for a prisoner exchange or other hints of his apprehension were received from the Wehrmacht. Some local priests conducted a search for him in the region without finding any clues.

Lieutenant Icardi and his teammates continued their liaison activities. However, the loss of Major Hollohan represented not only a great personal tragedy but also a serious setback in OSS plans. The hope had been to establish a prestigious mission that could negotiate at highest levels with the CLNAI, first in the waning days of the war and then in the post-liberation period.

The puzzle surrounding Hollohan's disappearance has never been completely resolved. After the team's villa was ambushed, Lieutenant Icardi radioed Company D that Hollohan was killed in the assault. But a widely publicized Italian court case after the war charged and convicted Icardi, in absentia, of Hollohan's murder. It was alleged that he and his OG sergeant absconded with the operational funds, and then, after poisoning and shooting him, dumped him into a lake.

Six years after Hollohan's disappearance, his body was found. He had been shot twice in the head, zipped into his sleeping bag, and thrown into Lake Orta. A lurid story in the September 1951 issue of *True* magazine identified Icardi as the murderer. An internal investigation had cleared Icardi, yet a Pentagon press release confirmed the *True* story.

Allegations of political motives became a crucial element of the case. It was charged that Icardi favored supporting the Communist and other leftist partisan groups while Hollohan was depicted as a devout Catholic conservative opposed to assisting these groups. Hollohan, according to the prosecution's argument, had to be eliminated so that Icardi and his teammates could supply the Garibaldini without interference.

Reverberations of the case and its follow-up became front-page material in the United States and Italian presses during the decade following the war. The U.S. House Armed Services Committee held hearings. Icardi acquired Edward Bennett Williams as legal counsel and published his defense in a book, *American Master Spy*. The protracted legal battle ended in 1956 with an acquittal, still the object of dispute among informed observers. Although the controversy surrounding the Hollohan case cast a shadow on the OSS record in the waning days of the war and its immediate aftermath, it did not bring a halt to the many different operations under way as the year 1944 drew to a close.[33]

I have few precise recollections of that December, when, owing to the stand-down in partisan operations, there may have been a slight easing of the normal Special Operations workload. One quirky detail that I do remember is being asked to join a group of colleagues who were going to hear one of my favorite operas, *La Traviata*, in the royal opera house in the Caserta palace where AFHQ was headquartered. I wore my dress uniform for the special dinner at our mess and the opera itself. We drove in several cars from San Leucio to the big palace. After taking a seat along with my friends in one of the boxes, I waited eagerly for the curtain to part. What a surprise it was to see nothing at all on the stage except a Victrola, from which the opening strains emerged. We heard the entire opera on the long-playing records of the era. Even so, the sound of the music and the spectacular setting made such a wonderful impression that I have retained only the happiest memories of that evening.

One other event, which now seems an incongruous escape from my duties, was a day of skiing in the foothills of the Apennines, fairly accessible to Caserta. Good friends Nancy Thompson and Ellen Hart of the regimental Message Center and Charlie Stiassni of the Czech desk went along on this carefree outing. Where we came by equipment now escapes me. I do recall that the hill where we chose to ski was completely in its natural state. No tows! We had to climb up for each run down. I still enjoy the photos from that day.

These and other memorabilia remind me of the extraordinary nature of the brief time I shared with the other headquarters staff in Caserta. We were nowhere

Charlie Stiassni and me

From left, Ellen Hart, Nancy Thompson, me

near the front lines and totally out of harm's way—indeed, living very comfortably—but our daily responsibilities were life or death concerns for the agents in the field and the Allied forces we supported. It was a heady and exhilarating period. As the year came to a close, I had no idea of the even greater responsibilities I would be given in the months ahead.

5

Caserta, 1945
1 January to 15 July 1945

*T*he winter stand-down of partisan activity eased the Operations Section's workload slightly, but our small staff had all we could handle in coordinating OSS contacts with the CLNAI in northern Italy. There was a high volume of these contacts, and in a 17 January memorandum to all branches, executive officer Norman Newhouse ordered the Operations Section to maintain the central file on them.[1]

Fifty-eight years after Newhouse issued that memo, Albert Materazzi discovered this file in the archives and led me to it. I was amazed to find how heavily involved in these dealings I was. My name appears repeatedly as an originator, a recipient, or an action officer in the daily flood of cable traffic, memos, and official reports. A review of the file today reveals the complexity of events rushing ahead in the confusion of war. Finding these records helped me greatly in recalling my small part in the grand scheme of the Allied campaign in Italy as it wound down to the German capitulation.

The CLNAI was the only resistance organization to receive Allied recognition and financial support, yet its clandestine base in northern Italy was far from secure. A 26 January cable from Baker, in Annemasse, to Glavin and me confirmed earlier reports that Ferrucio Parri had been captured on New Year's Eve in Milan. Parri was head of the Action Party, co-commander of CLNAI, and its most prominent spokesman. Baker's cable warned that if Maurizio (Parri's codename) talked to his captors, the entire status of the CLNAI might be jeopardized. Moreover, Baker assumed that there would be increased German patrols of the area surrounding Annemasse, partly due to Maurizio's capture.[2]

A small man with a huge shock of white hair, Parri was an idealistic veteran of the anti-Fascist cause who had been in and out of Mussolini's jails since 1927. Donald Downes described him as the "perfect symbol of resistance to policeism, stateism, and brutality."[3] Soon after his return to Milan from meetings in Caserta, he was apprehended in the house of another man whom the Germans were tracking and was held captive for more than two months, until 8 March. Because the Allies recognized Parri as a man of consequence and principles who would play an important role in Italian affairs after the war, they advised his captors through covert channels that he should be treated with respect and specifically warned against subjecting him to the torture often used in German prisons. As detailed below, he became a central figure in the efforts of Allen Dulles, an OSS representative in Berne, Switzerland, to negotiate an early surrender of the Nazis. After the war, Parri was elected Italy's first prime minister.

Meanwhile, in the French Savoy, there was a growing movement to annex Italian territory formerly under French rule. The Val d'Aosta, a magnificent Alpine area at Italy's extreme northwest frontier, was a prime target of the annexationists, because the main railway link between Italy and France ran through it. German troops had driven about a thousand Italian partisans out of the valley into France. In addition, a large number of Italian civilian refugees had fled Italy, across the border farther south. Many Italians were being held in French garrisons. French attitudes toward their neighbors, never very friendly, reached new levels of animosity after Mussolini crossed the border and even occupied parts of France. The CLNAI leadership had to cope not only with ruthless German occupiers in Italy but also with French territorial aspirations after the end of hostilities.

In early February, I made my first visit to Florence to consult with Colonel Suhling, who had moved his headquarters from Siena.[4] The battle for the liberation of Florence had been fought six months before my arrival. As the Allies approached the perimeter, the Germans proclaimed Florence an open city whose historic buildings and monuments were to be preserved. However, once the Allies entered the city, the Germans disregarded that declaration and destroyed almost a third of the medieval section. The Ponte Vecchio was the only bridge across the Arno that was left standing. Moreover, demolition charges that retreating Germans set at each end severely damaged the bridge, leaving huge piles of rubbish, burying many residents, and making the bridge inaccessible to advancing Allied troops. Most of the thirteenth- and fourteenth-century houses lining the Arno were also reduced to rubble. Even the baptistry attached to the Duomo was shelled.

In the fierce battle for the city, U.S. and New Zealand troops fought the Germans and their Italian cohorts, the black-shirted Republican Fascists. The Allies received invaluable support from Italian guerrillas, especially bands of the Garibaldi Brigade (or Garibaldini), a Communist formation named after the famous revolutionary firebrand of the 1800s. North of the city, the Wehrmacht maintained its principal defensive position along the heavily fortified Gothic Line. I saw the scars of battle everywhere in Florence, but recovery and rebuilding were already well under way.

Before the Allies entered the city, the Germans had conducted a wholesale looting of Florentine art treasures from the Uffizi, Pitti Palace, and other museums. Hitler and the top Wehrmacht generals intended to have all these works installed in their collections after they had won the war. At the time of my visit, little was known about the fate of these masterpieces, and the museums were closed. The OSS would play an important role in the recovery of the loot after VE Day.

Like other OSS personnel staying in Florence, I was billeted at the five-star Excelsior Hotel, my first taste of Italian luxury since Capri. This visit began my lifelong love affair with Florence. Even though Allied troops faced the challenge of breaching the Gothic Line when spring arrived, there were glimmers of hope that the end of the war was in sight. Florence was coming back to life, and the Florentines gave their American liberators the warmest possible reception.

My discussions with Colonel Suhling, Maj. Judson Smith, and other Company D officers involved two major issues: first, mitigating the Franco-Italian border dispute, and, second, planning for future meetings with CLNAI heads. With Parri now a prisoner of the Germans, leadership was in the hands of Parri's co-chairman, Luigi Longo, head of the Communist forces in northern Italy who, after years of exile in Russia, was considered a tool of Moscow. The military leader of the CLNAI, the politically neutral General Cadorna, had the nearly impossible task of mediating bitter disputes between the various factions, ranging from pro-monarchy to Communist partisan groups. Since Longo and Cadorna were both living under cover in Milan, our best contact with a CLNAI leader on our side of the lines was Dr. Eugenio Dugoni.

Dr. Dugoni was the CLN's official representative to French military and political authorities for mediating the Franco-Italian border dispute and especially the future of the Val d'Aosta. General de Gaulle, always ready to expand French dominion, added fuel to the fire by endorsing a petition—for circulation among the people of Val d'Aosta—to have the territory annexed to France. Dugoni had the delicate task of ensuring that the Italian resistance would help in resolving the dispute at the end of the war.

In fact, during most of the German occupation, partisans in regions bordering the Val d'Aosta had been able to rally the local citizenry in subversive measures, preventing the Fascists from fully controlling their homeland. The few Fascist officials on the scene could not enforce their own laws; people lived by partisan laws and collected partisan taxes. These regions were virtually autonomous.

OSS Detachment F, at Annemasse, close to the French-Italian border, was on the edge of this explosive situation. The detachment was using manback transportation to supply the Italian partisans with food and ammunition for sabotage and was also providing intelligence on current military positions and potential post-hostilities problems.

In addition to his role as emissary to the French, Dugoni was empowered as an intermediary to deal with Allied military commands and OSS representatives in this looming dispute. In this capacity, he traveled frequently between Caserta, Rome, and Florence. Another Dugoni priority was persuading Italian partisans who had escaped to France to return to Italy and fight the Germans. Several hundred had taken refuge on the western side of the border. The Allied command ultimately adopted the Dugoni approach when, on 29 March, Gen. Mark Clark called on all Italian partisans in France to return home and make their maximum contribution to the "complete and imminent liberation of their country."[5]

The Italian government had given Dugoni about one ton of cigarettes to be distributed to partisans, a well-intentioned if bizarre expression of official gratitude. Two cables in the CLN file indicate that I was available to escort Dugoni and the cigarettes, flying from Caserta to Lyon. Indeed, there are travel orders in my personal file to proceed to Rome, Florence, Annemasse, and Paris on or about 23 February. To the best of my recollection, that trip never took place, and I cannot remember what happened to the cigarettes. Indeed, events were moving so fast, and my memory of them is so blurred, that I have relied primarily on the recommendation for my Bronze Star award as a source for this period. It indicates that I was responsible for keeping the Annemasse base supplied with the skis, arms, and other materials needed for their cross-border operations and for disseminating their intelligence on Franco-Italian disputes to military authorities at SHAEF, AFHQ, and 15th Army Group. It also states that it was largely due to the efforts of Captain Kloman (I had been promoted in April) that the detachment in Annemasse was established.[6]

While the military advance was stalled during January and February 1945, top priority was given to preparations for the spring campaign. Allied resupply of the partisans reached a peak during those two months. All branches of the OSS prepared to provide the most effective support to the military, once the campaign was launched. Plans were also being made to deal with the political situation that would arise in the aftermath of a ceasefire.

One element of such Allied planning was codenamed Rankin B, a British-initiated proposal for the stationing of designated Allied officers at strategic posts in northern cities to take over local administration in the event that German retreat left a power vacuum. A major goal of Rankin was to prevent Communist takeovers of local governments. Within the OSS, it was suspected that the plan was actually a scheme for British Special Operations Executive (SOE) officers to take control and pursue British Foreign Office policies in support of the pro-monarchist forces. The OSS lacked the manpower to staff this project and decided not to take part in the Rankin plan.[7]

Another case in which British-American cooperation gave way to rivalry occurred in the matter of pinpoints for drop zones in March, when both nations were competing to send teams behind enemy lines. The British No. 1 Special Force had requested a list of OSS pinpoints for drop zones. The United States declined to provide the list because Secret Intelligence (SI), which ran the greatest number of OSS teams, insisted that their teams' locations not be divulged. Somehow, however, the British gained enough information about coordinates of OSS pinpoints that they began dropping teams blind into OSS drop zones without advance notice or permission. This risky practice was potentially very disruptive and confusing for the partisans at the drop zones, who feared that their locations might be divulged. Moreover, on a few occasions the OSS requested No. 1 Special Force to provide reception for OSS teams, but the British generally found some reason why they could not do so. Teamwork between the two air supply units was being severely strained.[8]

Such incidents were at odds with the earlier pattern of cooperation, which the OSS Air Operations review officer properly acknowledged in a postwar report. He stressed the usually high level of teamwork between the two Allied partners, and the professionalism of British officers in the competitive bidding for aviation resources.[9]

During March, Dugoni was involved in discussions with OSS representatives and Allied military commanders who were dealing with the evolving military and political situation. Included in these talks were Col. John Riepe, G-3 Operations; and Gen. Alfred Gruenther, Gen. Mark Clark's chief of staff. Through these talks, Dugoni came to realize that the top leadership in Allied commands was inadequately informed about the resistance movement, its importance to the military campaign, and the problems that could arise after a ceasefire. He warned of difficulties if the partisans rejected Allied efforts to take away their arms. Such resistance, Dugoni observed, was likely unless the partisans were assured of an adequate program of "epuration," literally a purging of pro-Fascist elements of the population. Much as the partisans hated the Germans, they held their own collaborating countrymen in even greater contempt. Furthermore, they felt that the Fascists in southern Italy had not been adequately punished for their traitorous actions. Dugoni warned that partisans in northern Italy were already planning their own purges at the war's end.

General Gruenther asked about the danger of a Communist uprising after a German retreat. Dugoni responded that he considered such a development unlikely—but, he warned prophetically, irresponsible elements could resort to rebellion if anti-Fascist purges were not quickly conducted.[10]

Later that month, after debating where Dugoni could be most useful in postwar discussions, he chose to be dropped into France. There he could cross the Italian border readily at the time of a ceasefire. On 9 April 1945, despite his lack of jump training, Dugoni was successfully dropped to an SI Orange team. A man of great courage, he was high on General Donovan's list of partisans to receive letters of appreciation.

A break in the weather in early March had allowed the aerial resupply program to drop larger volumes (some 175,000 pounds in two weeks) to the partisans.

At the same time, a marked increase in both the volume and quality of intelligence from OSS operations in northern Italy was gaining converts in G-2 sections of the military forces. A propitious moment had arrived for parachuting in missions to train the partisans how to use explosives and commando tactics. The first to go were two Operational Group (OG) teams, Santee and Spokane, dropped to SI reception committees on 4 March. The OGs were under the command of their chief, Col. Russell Livermore, with Capt. Albert Materazzi as their operations officer.[11]

OSS-led partisan teams and those of our British counterpart were proving to be increasingly valuable to the military campaign with many calls each day for bombing strikes on specific targets. If a team observed a railroad yard containing a sizable number of railcars and locomotives, the coordinates of the site would be reported along with a call for a strike at a given time. Usually within twenty-four to thirty-six hours the target would be destroyed or badly damaged. With the proliferation of such attacks, the tide of battle began to turn.

Allen Dulles had assumed the key position of OSS representative in Berne in November 1942 with the title special assistant to the American minister, a cover widely recognized in intelligence circles as the only way to account for his presence in neutral Switzerland. He was uniquely qualified, having served in the same city twenty-five years earlier as a junior Foreign Service officer. Subsequently he served on the staff of the American Commission in Berlin where he came to know many German industrialists and military leaders. His career as an international lawyer brought him into contact with a wide range of European businessmen and political leaders. During World War II his insider's knowledge of the German establishment was essential in his continuing efforts to promote the most promising plots to overthrow Hitler. His connections qualified him to orchestrate the elaborate plans for achieving an early German surrender in Italy, codenamed Sunrise.

Dulles was also running certain operations in northern Italy in some of the same areas where Italian SI, SO, and OG teams were operating. As these teams carried out their work with the Italian resistance, some jurisdictional confusion was created. Milton Katz, deputy chief of SI, headed a committee that met in Caserta in early February to propose ways to clarify the situation. Their principal recommendation, soon implemented, was to send a trusted mediator, Emilio Daddario, to Switzerland to work with Allen Dulles and his chief assistant, Don Jones. Daddario served as a representative of all OSS Italy branches. He and Jones worked together to set up better communications between Dulles's office, OSS offices in Florence, Company D, and regimental headquarters in Caserta. Daddario maintained regular radio contact with Company D, which in turn coordinated with 15th Army Group, now under the command of Gen. Mark Clark.

As the military front advanced up the peninsula, it became necessary for OSS units to deploy northward. On 19 February, the day when Daddario arrived in Switzerland, Max Corvo led a long truck convoy that moved all SI Brindisi equipment and personnel to Siena.

The following narrative is a greatly condensed synopsis of Sunrise's history, based on my review of the many accounts published after the war. Allen Dulles's history of these events, *The Secret Surrender,* published in 1966, provided the perspective of the mastermind of the negotiations. His book tells of the high expectations at the initiation of the surrender planning, the powerful figures on both sides of the war whose cooperation was required for success, and the complexities involved in assembling all the pieces to finish the task.[12]

A small, select group of senior OSS officials and top military officers took part in the plan that Dulles had been waiting to implement when the time was right. The principal benefit anticipated from the project was to greatly reduce the number of Allied casualties. Other goals of the Sunrise planners included the assurance of a bloodless transition from war to peace, along with the prevention of the kind of leftist revolt that followed Britain's withdrawal from Greece. There was ample reason for concern that after a ceasefire, pro-Communists in the northern Italian populace would conspire with the strong Communist representation in the resistance to take control of local jurisdictions throughout the north.

As early as 1943, OSS Berne had received reports of wavering within enemy commands in Italy, and in the early months of 1944, Berne was advising Washington of rifts. Of particular note were those between the old *Oberkommando der Wehrmacht* (OKW) and Hitler's Secret Service (SS). Dulles and his staff believed that Allied commands were seriously overestimating the German will to resist. They had little success in convincing Washington and London to pursue what they regarded as opportunities to drive a wedge between factions of the German military establishment. British intelligence was particularly skittish about overtures from the enemy, having been burned too often by following false leads that alleged defectors had offered.

In late 1944, as the Germans dug in for the winter behind their formidable Gothic Line, doubts must have been spreading within their ranks about their ability to hold their Italian bastion. Top Nazi commands were concerned not only about the future of their troops if they were forced to an unconditional surrender, but also about the possible political vacuum created by withdrawal of the Wehrmacht. They were, as well, as aware as the Allies that northern Italy was ripe for a Communist takeover. The fear of a Stalinist push, starting in Yugoslavia and crossing onto the Istrian peninsula, had a more chilling effect on some of Hitler's generals than did the prospect of an Allied occupation.

In November 1944, an OSS team in Venice reported a German feeler expressing a desire to surrender. This was followed by a series of feelers sent to both Berne and Company D of OSS. These feelers proposed detailed arrangements for conferences and conditions for surrender, but they were not considered of sufficient authority to pursue. Then in late January 1945 a directive relayed from Washington warned all OSS teams that no terms could be accepted other than unconditional surrender and that the teams themselves could undertake no negotiations. Company D would be the channel for transmitting all surrender feelers from the field to the Allied Command.

That same month, Dulles received another peace overture, this one delivered through the Catholic Church and Italian industrialist channels. He was not impressed because this proposal seemed to stem from a low level of the SS rather than the top German command. A second approach from a rich industrialist, Baron Luigi Parilli, also failed at first to sway Dulles. However, when Parilli convinced him that he represented Gen. Karl Wolff, the top SS commander in all of Italy, Dulles considered it worth exploring. Wolff had served as Heinrich Himmler's personal adjutant and reported directly to him from his Italian command. Dulles conceived a cunning test of authenticity. He requested the release of Ferrucio Parri, still a captive in Milan. The Germans, having previously received the Allied warnings to respect his seniority and status, correctly surmised that the Allies were slating Parri for leadership after the war. The Nazis calculated that it would be to their advantage to release him. Parri arrived in Switzerland on 8 March, in the custody of an SS captain. At this point, Dulles and his top-secret planning group began to take more seriously the possibility of negotiating surrender.

Soon after the meeting with Parri, Dulles rushed off to a meeting with General Wolff, who had arrived in Zurich along with Baron Parilli. In order to persuade Dulles to meet with him, Wolff had sent a remarkable communiqué that included his resume and a recitation of his "good deeds," actions he thought would convince Dulles of his value as a dealmaker. By this time, the OSS had intelligence indicating that one of Wolff's many responsibilities was overseeing the custody of the huge volume of Florentine art treasures that the Germans had confiscated. Much to the amazement of Dulles and his staff, Wolff sent a lengthy and carefully documented list identifying each of these treasures along with his promise to deliver them.[13]

The day after Parri's arrival in Berne, Dulles received an unexpected message from Allied headquarters saying that two senior AFHQ staff officers were on their way to Berne with a contingent of OSS staff personnel to begin the second phase of Sunrise. There followed a ten-day lull before individuals empowered to negotiate could be assembled. Then on 13 March 1945 American general Lyman Lemnitzer and British general Terence Airey, in civilian disguise, met with Gen. Karl Wolff on the Swiss-Italian border. Accompanying them was David Crockett, manager of OSS operational funds in Caserta. After that session, Wolff had to return to his Italian headquarters in Bolzano to sound out his superiors while the Allied generals went to Lyon.

During the ten-day lull, two representatives of the CLNAI arrived in Berne for a strategy meeting that the OSS and SOE had requested weeks earlier. Dulles wanted to keep the partisans from knowing about the surrender plan, fearing that their allegiance to the Allied cause would be undermined. Therefore, he sent them on to talk with Lemnitzer and Airey in Lyon. Avoiding talk of surrender, the two Allied generals brought up their concern about a Communist-led revolution. By this time, AFHQ knew that a contingent of Russian officers with official Soviet army credentials had crossed the Yugoslav border and was already working with the Communist Garibaldini. The CLN envoys tried to convince the generals that despite the strength of the Garibaldini, the Greek debacle would not be repeated.

Negotiations resumed on 19 March when Generals Lemnitzer and Airey again met with General Wolff at the Swiss border town of Ascona. After what was regarded as a productive meeting Wolff again returned to his headquarters to sound out the Wehrmacht commanders. However, once again negotiations were stalled, this time for nearly an entire month by two major complications. General Wolff ran into objections from his superiors in Berlin. Some of Hitler's inner circle sought to portray Wolff as untrustworthy and too willing to cave in to the Allies. Furthermore, a suspicious Soviet government was signaling concerns about any American-British initiative that might interfere with their plans to move west from Yugoslavia.

When the Soviets were first informed of the possibility of peace negotiations, Foreign Minister Molotov indicated that Russia wanted to dispatch three Red Army officers immediately to join in the talks. The Allies, realizing that Russian involvement would delay the negotiations, rejected the offer by saying that at this preliminary stage, no point would be served, and that if they did attend, they could be there only as observers. Molotov fired back that under this condition, the Russians chose not to send anyone. Very soon thereafter another Molotov message demanded that the talks be called off if the Russians could not participate.

President Franklin Roosevelt, in a telegram seeking to placate Stalin, recounted some of the history of the talks to date while intentionally leaving out the fact that two Allied generals had already initiated negotiations in Switzerland. When Stalin was finally informed *ex post facto* that talks had been held, he erupted in a note to British ambassador Eden, in Moscow, expressing great displeasure that his allies had been working for two weeks "behind the back of the Soviet Union."[14]

On 10 April the Allies launched their big spring offensive, prompting partisans throughout the Po Valley to incite widespread insurrection. Led by some seventy OSS teams, about fifty thousand partisans attacked German forces from the rear. The partisans blew up bridges, ambushed convoys, and cleared entire areas of German troops. Although General Clark called on them to be patient until the right time for an uprising, a CLN proclamation in Milan called for German and Fascist forces "to surrender or perish." Parri, returning from consultations in Caserta, advised his comrades that the Allies appeared less interested in the partisan cause and more concerned about the danger of a left-wing revolution and the sabotaging of power plants and other parts of the industrial infrastructure.

After having written a conciliatory note to Stalin, President Roosevelt died on the morning of 12 April 1945. He had indicated that what he called the Berne incident, an intentionally vague reference to Sunrise, had faded into the past without having accomplished anything of significance. Roosevelt's death, aside from its devastating effect on the entire Allied war effort, left the direction of U.S. participation in Sunrise virtually leaderless. Vice President Truman had not been briefed on the significance of the surrender talks. Moreover, events in Italy were rushing to a conclusion. On 19 April, Bologna fell to the partisans, who handed it over to advancing Allied troops. A Communist mayor was speedily elected. To coordinate partisan uprisings throughout the north, CLNAI formed the Insurrection Committee, headed by Luigi Longo, leader of the pro-Communist brigades. It announced that all captured Fascist officials were subject to execution.

On 20 April, Dulles was ordered by Washington to break off all surrender negotiations because Churchill and the senior American military command were unwilling to risk alienating the Soviets for what were still deemed questionable German overtures. Dulles was explicitly ordered not to continue the German contacts he had cultivated. Sorely disappointed, he was even more frustrated when three days later General Wolff and a top Wehrmacht officer appeared unexpectedly at the Swiss border, prepared to sign for surrender of all German forces in northern Italy. Dulles had to keep the Nazis waiting while urgently seeking instructions from Washington. On 24 April, the first American units crossed the Po River, setting off a signal for spontaneous popular uprisings in all the northern industrial centers.

Dulles decided that, in the absence of instructions from Washington, the best course was to urge General Wolff to return to his headquarters with the difficult assignment of maintaining order within the Nazi ranks and averting violence. En route to Bolzano, Wolff stopped off in a villa thirty miles north of Milan, which was soon surrounded by armed partisans. He managed to get word of his predicament to Dulles, who determined that Wolff was so crucial to his surrender plans that he should be rescued. One of the most incongruous and daring rescue efforts of the war was mounted as the OSS sought to free a German

general, in command of some of the most feared and ruthless troops, from capture by partisans supporting the Allied cause. The operation involved, among
others, a diverse cast of partisan bands, a cardinal who had long been seeking to
arrange a peace, two SS officials from the now-dissolved German border patrol,
Dulles's assistant Donald Jones, and the naturalized American Gero von Schulze
Gaevernitz, Dulles's old friend and right-hand man. Wolff was extricated. After
switching into civilian clothes, he proceeded to Bolzano.

Meanwhile, Emilio (Mim) Daddario had been assigned the vitally important task of capturing the top Fascist leadership to prevent the partisans
from executing them before they were brought to trial. On 26 April 1945,
Daddario and a small armed group crossed the Swiss border, heading for Lake
Como and seeking not only to round up the Fascist leaders, including Mussolini,
but also to arrange a cessation of hostilities to prevent unnecessary bloodshed.
Accompanied by the Italian partisan lieutenant Bonetti, Daddario walked under a white flag toward the villa Locatelli, which housed the top German command seeking to negotiate a ceasefire. The goal was an agreement that the
German troops would surrender to the first Allied troops to arrive and that
Marshal Rodolfo Graziani, chief of staff of the Italian Republic's armed forces,
would be handed over with his party as Daddario's prisoners. An angry group
of six armed socialist guerrillas demanded that the Americans hand over the
Fascist marshal so that they could dispose of him, but Daddario placed himself
in front of them unarmed and declared that they would have to eliminate him
first. The frustrated partisans backed down, muttering bloody oaths against
American coddling of the Fascists.

With Graziani and his party dispatched under guard in a five-car convoy,
Daddario proceeded to Como, where trouble was brewing in a stadium that held
a large contingent of armed German soldiers. Even though they increasingly realized that hostilities were virtually at an end, some restless Germans were on the
verge of provoking a general disturbance. In a meeting with General Leyers, their
commander, Daddario secured an agreement that all troops would remain in the
stadium to await surrender to the first Allied troops while three-quarters of their
arms would be immediately set aside for delivery to the Allies. Partisan guards
would be regularized and would patrol, at a certain distance from the stadium, to
prevent any undue incidents. Thus, in these several encounters, Daddario and
his teammates succeeded in stabilizing an extremely explosive situation.

Meanwhile, the OSS learned that Mussolini had fled to Lake Como and
was hiding, with his chief ministers, not far from the villa where Wolff had been
held. Il Duce's mistress, Claretta Petacci, had come to be at his side. He tried
various ploys to arrange favorable terms for surrender, either with the CLNAI or
with Dulles in Berne, but Dulles was not about to offer Mussolini a chance to
enter a neutral country and obtain asylum.

Mussolini's group made a bungled attempt to cross the border into Switzerland, but a band of partisans captured them and put them in the custody of a squad of Communists led by Col. Walter Audisio. This partisan officer was part of a Garibaldini brigade that an OSS Operational Group had armed and trained. Most of the Garibaldini group had cooperated fully with the OSS team but Audisio remained a renegade.

Uncertainty surrounds exactly what transpired. The Max Corvo version of events holds that on the afternoon of 28 April Audisio and Aldo Lampredi, vice-chief of the Garibaldini brigade, executed Il Duce and his mistress and transported their bodies to Milan. Another version absolves Audisio and Lampredi of any involvement, alleging that angry partisans were responsible. Whoever conducted the execution, the rash action corresponded with the mob's pent-up anger, though it violated the Allied instruction that Mussolini was to be captured alive and turned over to a military tribunal. The three other members of Mussolini's party were executed in the town square of the village of Dongo. The Gestapo command post in Milan was surrounded by belligerent partisans pressing for orders to attack, and the delicate task of mediating between the Gestapo chief and partisan leaders fell to Daddario, who had been joined by Aldo Icardi, deputy to the late Captain Hollohan and, allegedly, his murderer.

On 19 April, the bodies of the five Fascists were hung upside down from the roof of a gas station in central Milan. Thousands of Italians filed by in festive mood to view the gory end of this hated troop. The Allies did not condemn the partisan action, and indeed it had the beneficial effect of satisfying, to some degree, the demand for the purging of collaborators. However, angry crowds throughout the north continued to seek retribution against Fascist collaborators, who were now on the defensive.[15]

On 28 April, Washington again reversed itself and resurrected Sunrise, stipulating that the surrender document was to be signed at AFHQ Caserta with an effective date of 2:00 PM on 2 May. Preparing for that deadline involved many complicated logistical and diplomatic tasks to ensure that all signers and their staffs were assembled and that the document itself was ready for signature. Although the surrender plans had long been an open secret, a three-day news embargo was decreed to prevent obstruction of the process before official announcement of the surrender terms. Allen Dulles, widely known as the late president's personal representative, did not go to Caserta, because it was felt that his presence would attract too much attention to the still-secret arrangements. Instead, Gero von Schulze Gaevernitz went and served in the dual role of interpreter and negotiator. His negotiating skills were a great asset in overcoming the Germans' last-minute reservations about a number of the surrender's terms.

Signing for the Allies was Lt. Gen. W. D. Morgan, chief of staff for Field Marshal Sir Harold Alexander, Supreme Allied Commander, Mediterranean

Theater. The German signer was Viktor von Schweinitz, a lieutenant colonel in the General Staff. A small group of British and American press were invited to cover the event despite the ban on publicity, and they kept the secret for three days.

After Sunrise went into effect, Nazi troops that had not already surrendered to Allied or partisan forces began a piecemeal process of turning over their arms. General Wolff, in response to criticism from some of his superiors in Berlin, explained that his actions had prevented a Communist uprising that would have established a Soviet republic in northern Italy. Even though hostilities in Italy had effectively ceased, spasmodic flare-ups continued in the German heartland. The line of communications established through Sunrise was put to use in further surrender discussions.[16]

Dulles exulted in having overcome all the obstacles to his elaborate plans with the completion of the Sunrise formalities. Emerging from the heavy cloak of secrecy, he broke into the limelight of public acclaim and commendation from his peers. Only one episode dampened his enjoyment of the moment. Soon after the surrender signing, Dulles made a visit to the Milan headquarters of SI without prior notification, disregarding the internal agreement on boundaries between his terrain and that of OSS Italy. His appearance took Vincent Scamporino totally by surprise. Bad blood had developed between Dulles and the SI officials, partly over turf issues. For example, Corvo took exception when Dulles infiltrated his own radio operator to Wolff's Bolzano headquarters at a time when SI already had their own team, Norma, in place. But the underlying cause of tension may well have been personality clashes and colliding egos.

In describing the episode, Corvo cites Scamporino's annoyance at Dulles's failure to give advance notice of his visit, but he also points to Dulles's patronizing and autocratic attitude in his discussions of some jurisdictional matters. The meeting ended abruptly after Scamporino, living up to his reputation for rude behavior, infuriated Dulles with one of his typically blunt remarks. Dulles walked out the door, muttering that he had never been so humiliated in his life and vowing that SI would hear more about the matter that he had come to discuss. Indeed, Dulles did relay his negative comments about SI to General Donovan shortly thereafter, thus lending support to the decision for an early closing down of the entire SI branch.[17]

Back in the more compatible environment of Berne, Dulles was able to take satisfaction in the rapid succession of events following the surrender. VE Day came on 5 May, with the surrender of General Kesselring's Army Group G to the American Sixth Army Group under Gen. Jacob Devers. Hitler had committed suicide in his bunker on 30 April, but a week went by before Alfred Jodl, operations chief of the German high command, signed the official surrender of the Third Reich on 7 May.

The principal German player in Sunrise was destined for an unhappy fate. In the fall of 1945, Wolff was taken from internment in Italy to Nuremberg where he served for four years as a witness in certain of the major war-crime trials. When the question of his own complicity in the SS crimes was taken up, the evidence was not considered sufficient for conviction—initially. In 1964, a German court tried Wolff and found that his closeness to Himmler made him privy to SS actions and thus deeply entangled in the atrocities. Indeed, in 1942 he had signed a transportation order for railroad cars that took Jews to concentration camps. Wolff received a fifteen-year prison sentence.

Although he was a convicted war criminal, it should also be noted that Wolff contributed more than anyone else in the Wehrmacht to the final German surrender in Italy. Furthermore, on one important occasion, he defied Himmler's order instructing him to arrange for the transportation of the huge collection of Italian art treasures to Austria, where they would be beyond Wolff's control. These masterworks had been safely stored in underground tunnels in the Italian Tyrol, protected from looters or bomb damage. Wolff deserves credit for saving these works from an uncertain fate and making it possible for millions of art lovers to view them today, back in their original settings.

In the eight days following the surrender, General Wolff and his wife hosted a series of conferences and elegant dinners in the general's headquarters, the palace of the Duke of Pistoia in Bolzano. Countless champagne toasts were drunk to celebrate Wolff's forty-fifth birthday, in a surreal atmosphere of goodwill between former enemies. A remarkable cast of high-ranking German officers met with Gero von Schulze Gaevernitz, representing Dulles, and other OSS officials involved in Sunrise. Among these was Theodore Ryan, chief of the SI Reports Section in Caserta who had been assigned responsibility for securing the collection of Florentine art treasures. In fact, Wolff loaned his SS car and chauffeur to Ryan and Gaevernitz so they could drive to the small provincial courthouse where some of the art had been stored. All the Nazi-held art was turned over to the American Fifth Army, which on 20 July returned the treasures to Florence in a train of thirteen cargo cars.

Col. Russell Livermore, chief of the Operational Groups, was also in Bolzano, representing the 15th Army Group in interrogating Wolff. Livermore was seeking information on the fate of OSS personnel who had been captured behind enemy lines. After stalling a response to the inquiry, it was revealed that none of these individuals had survived. On 13 May, the Wolff celebratory entertainments came to an abrupt end when he and his German guests were lined up in his palace courtyard palace and loaded in American Army trucks to be taken to prisoner of war camps.

Despite all the efforts devoted to negotiating an early surrender, the final outcome of the Sunrise operation fell short of the high hopes generated

Front row, left to right, General Roettiger, Gaevernitz, Major Wenner, General Wolff, and Theodore Ryan in Bolzano, after surrender

at its outset. Instead of shortening the hostilities and reducing casualties by several weeks, the formal surrender came only a few days before the Wehrmacht's collapse. But even a few days of peace represented a significant achievement, especially to troops on the front lines. If Dulles had been able to carry out his plan on the timetable he had envisaged, it would have been a far greater achievement. Nearly two months elapsed between General Wolff's first proposed surrender and the 2 May signing, months marked by continued bloodshed, turbulence, and confusion in the north. Even such a well-connected and skillful organizer as Allen Dulles could not arrange all the pieces of the puzzle to achieve a settlement in his preferred timeline. He lacked the authority to control even the different factions in the OSS, each with its own agenda. Beyond that, he had to bring into his scheme President Roosevelt and Prime Minister Churchill; several very senior military commanders; leaders of the CLNAI, itself torn by ideological rivalries; and, last but not least, the representatives of the German military empowered to sign a surrender document.

The day of Kesselring's surrender, 5 May, was also the day I received orders to proceed to Florence.[18] During all the activity associated with Sunrise, I had been at my post in the Operations Section in Caserta. Although I was not in the inner circle of those involved in the negotiations, I was aware of Sunrise developments. Indeed, from travel orders in my file dated 17 February, it appears that I had been summoned for temporary duty in Switzerland, but this was another case of proposed travel that never happened.[19]

In early March 1945, just at the time when Parri's appearance in Berne had generated momentum for Sunrise, I had been promoted to the position of acting chief of Operations, OSS, Mediterranean Theater. The slot had remained vacant during the period since Colonel Davis's departure, and Lt. Col. Martin Wood had been appointed to it on 10 March. But Wood was ordered back to Washington only a week later, and Colonel Glavin needed to appoint someone to fill the sudden void. Despite my youth (twenty-three years old) and junior rank, Glavin appointed me, thus catapulting me into a midlevel executive position. Luckily, my good friend Bill Underwood was named as my deputy. We worked well together, and I never sensed any resentment on his part that I had been chosen for the top spot, even though I was several years his junior and he was well qualified for the position.

It amused me to see, on the official organization chart, that slots for a full Army colonel and a Navy captain were shown reporting to my position. Along with my exalted title went the most coveted car in the motor pool, a Lancia, chauffeured by one of our top drivers. Other OSS officers who far outranked me were not amused to see this junior officer being driven around in such style. Before long, the Lancia and driver were reassigned to a higher-ranking official.

During this period, I continued to represent the SO at AFHQ, especially at the regular G-3 Special Operations meetings dealing with partisan support operations and policy. The SO branch at this point had thirty-eight teams in northern Italy with a total of one hundred Italian agents, five American Army officers, and four enlisted men. Our office maintained a steady flow of cable traffic with the Operations office of Company D in Florence. We were not cleared to receive Sunrise traffic but continued in the liaison role with CLNAI, coordinating movement of its leaders from enemy-held territory to various locations in liberated Italy.

Bill Underwood and I, as the only two officers manning the SO desk, were swamped by the demands for maintaining our many contacts and keeping up with the fast-moving events of the war. However, our situation was probably typical for most desks in Caserta headquarters, and we found our job exhilarating. Now, in retrospect, I realize that our responsibilities far exceeded our level of preparation.

My orders to go to Florence were dated 5 May, but I cannot recall the specific purpose of the travel. OSS travel orders, always classified and written expressly to conceal their real purpose, do not reveal what the mission is expected to accomplish. In this case, the orders read simply: "for the purpose of accomplishing an assigned mission." Undoubtedly, I was expected to consult with Colonel Suhling and Major Smith, chief of Operations, who would have been overwhelmed in the chaotic aftermath of the ceasefire.

I do recall that once again I was billeted in the splendid Excelsior. My most vivid memory is a concert in which the national anthems of all the Allied countries were played. The Allies providing troops for the Italian campaign included a great number of countries other than the United States and Great Britain. Among what were sometimes called "the lesser Allies" were New Zealand, whose troops played such a vital role in liberating Florence, Canada, Poland, India, Brazil, Morocco, Czechoslovakia, and others. I particularly remember hearing for the first time the Czech national anthem, *The Moldau*. Since that day in Florence, every time I hear this piece I am transported back to the ballroom of the Excelsior.

Our private victory celebrations lasted several days, but the euphoria gave way to a strange sense of anticlimax. President Roosevelt's death was still being mourned. Mixed emotions prevailed, as we faced up to the unfinished war against Japan and the realization that associations formed in our secret Caserta hideaway were coming to an end. Knowing that we would soon be scattering to various destinations all over the globe took some of the pleasure away from the promise of returning home. Closing our offices was a letdown after the excitement of the tasks we had been performing. In addition to the paperwork associated with personnel reassignment, the disposal of files, and winding down of radio contacts, all branches of the organization were ordered to prepare histories of their activities. The main purpose of these records was to document lessons learned from experience that could be applied to the future.

Bill Underwood and I, as the only officers at Caserta Operations, were assigned the task of writing the regimental Operations Section history. To remove us from distractions, we were ordered to Capri for several days. Needless to say, we welcomed the assignment to such an idyllic location and one so appropriate for our task. The island and the Villa Fortini had figured so prominently in the early phases of the Italian invasion. Though Mrs. Harrison Williams and General Donovan had envisioned the villa as a site for R and R, Underwood and I took our writing assignment seriously. We worked hard every day with little time for either R or R. But our efforts were lost to posterity. After the war, I tried to find out what happened to our report, but it seems to have been lost in the huge volume of documents shipped from overseas posts back to Washington. When I began my search in the archives, the most useful history that I did find was that written by the Operations Section of Company D.[20]

Naturally, each branch of the OSS wanted to claim as much as possible in the way of accomplishments. Given the confusion of war, the secrecy in which OSS units operated, and the natural human tendency to exaggerate achievements, it is not surprising that the postwar histories presented different versions of events. In fact, when Kermit Roosevelt compiled his comprehensive OSS history, he was instructed not to include the names of individuals. This was because of concern that there would be too much contention about who had accomplished what. Roosevelt himself deplored this constriction on his writing, but it may have prevented endless disputes after the war about his account. Indeed, the disagreements came to a head even as the branch histories were being written.

One example of this is a memorandum to the regimental secretariat that I cosigned with my counterpart in Company D, Maj. Judson Smith, criticizing a report entitled "Italian SI Achievements in the Last Phase of the Italian Campaign." Our memo, while acknowledging the great value of SI's role, charges that faulty data are presented and that SI accomplishments are overemphasized, almost totally ignoring those of other branches. In retrospect, this document seems to suggest that headquarters officers such as Jud Smith and I were seeking to ensure recognition of the accomplishments of their respective branches while losing sight of the inter-branch cooperation that usually prevailed in the field.[21]

The Smith-Kloman memo was written just sixteen days before the SI was ordered to liquidate completely. The SI's many achievements had gained wide recognition, not least from General Donovan himself, who had great respect for Corvo, Scamporino, and their colleagues. But the SI had also alienated too many people in high places, and they wanted to see the branch closed down. Allen Dulles, having tangled with the outspoken Scamporino in Milan after Sunrise, was only one of the influential critics. Donovan was fighting on two fronts—one against charges of permitting Communists to serve in his organization, and the other to ensure the continuation of a central intelligence organization after the war. Thus embattled, he was less able to protect his friends. Corvo writes in his book that when he asked Donovan why he had been recalled to Washington in July, Donovan answered, "You Italians have politics in your blood . . . and you and Scamp were getting mixed up in Italian politics."[22]

However, the more likely reason for SI's untimely termination and Corvo's abrupt exit was resentment and jealousy among peers. This resulted, in part, from the failure of top SI leaders to instill a sense of teamwork and from their insistence on claiming all the credit for the entire organization's accomplishments. Corvo's book is a case in point. Published forty-five years after the war's end, it is a valuable record that meticulously documents day-to-day events all through the Italian campaign. I relied on it heavily for this memoir. However, the book's title, *The OSS in Italy*, implies that the SI story that Corvo tells is the whole OSS story, or at least the only one worth telling.

After VE Day and the shift in OSS attention from Europe to the Far East, it was time to close down Italian operations while also expressing American gratitude to the partisans and all the political figures who had risked their lives in helping to defeat the Germans. General Donovan issued detailed instructions to the principal officers of OSS Italy for letters of appreciation.

As an inducement for those who had been called on to serve behind enemy lines, some of the first recruits had been promised two hundred dollars a month in salaries, plus a five-thousand-dollar life insurance policy. Those partisans who were able to collect on these promises were greatly disappointed when payment was made at the legal exchange rate rather than that of the much higher black market. Partisans also received an impressive parchment certificate with a red seal and signed by General Donovan expressing sincere gratitude for the recipient's aid to the United States Army in the battle for the liberation of Italy. Unfortunately, some of these fell into the hands of ex-Fascists who used them to their own advantage.[23]

On 20 June, Colonel Glavin authorized travel orders instructing two colleagues and me to proceed to eight cities in the north: Rome, Florence, Milan, Turin, Bolzano, Verona, Venice, Genoa, and such other places in Italy as might be necessary "for the purpose of accomplishing an assigned mission."[24] The two other recipients of these orders were Lt. Col. Stewart McKenney and Patricia Malmstedt. As executive officer to the colonel heading G-3 Special Operations AFHQ, McKenney had been one of my principal contacts at the regular AFHQ meetings in Caserta. I had also served under him in Algiers, where he had authorized my very short jump-training course. Patricia Malmstedt was the disbursing officer in the OSS regimental financial office.

Our "assigned mission" was to meet with key figures of the partisan resistance who had served as OSS agents, expressing appreciation for their services, delivering certificates and, in some cases, their financial compensation. For example, we met in Venice with Pietro Ferraro, one of the most productive agents of the Goff chain who had headed the Margot-Hollis mission in the Veneto region. His team had transmitted the messages forewarning the Eighth Army of Tito's plan to occupy Trieste, which had resulted in the movement of the New Zealand Division into the area and forced the withdrawal of the Yugoslavs. However, most of our time on this mission might more accurately be called R and R, or an elegant vacation. Stewart McKenney's friend Air Force colonel Burt Andrus had been assigned a plane and pilot for a five-day period to go anywhere in Italy that he chose. Andrus invited McKenney to accompany him, and I also was invited to join the group. The photos that I kept in my scrapbook speak for themselves. Most of our time was spent at a villa on Lake Como.

On the Grand Canal, Venice (I am at left), with John H. McLeod, Patricia Malmstedt, Pietro Ferraro, Burt Andrus, and (at top) Luisa Guarniera

Something was in the air with the winding down of the war, and our Caserta contingent contemplated what would always be remembered as one of the precious moments of our lives. June was busting out all over, as we heard on broadcasts of the hit Broadway musical *Carousel*. We realized how exceptionally lucky we had been—thrown together in an almost idyllic setting, incongruously to support a bloody war against a ruthless enemy. Between writing histories and packing up offices, we found time for sailing in the Bay of Naples, motoring to Sorrento and Amalfi, and socializing with friends.

It was hardly surprising that four attractive couples became engaged or were actually married during this period. Each had conducted their courtships in the romantic setting of the southern Italian littoral. David Crockett, the wizard overseer of OSS European currencies and manager of our operational funds, became engaged to Marian Yates. Bill Maddox, the brilliant professor of political scientist turned chief of SI, married Louise Hepburn. Col. Ellery Huntington, the aging but still swashbuckling chief of the OSS mission to Tito, married Kitty du Bois. Col. Stewart McKenney, deputy to the chief of G-3 AFHQ, married Patricia Malmstedt.

With Patricia Malmstedt, Lake Como

Two other romantic liaisons were under way at top levels of regimental headquarters involving members of the WACs, the Women's Army Corps, assigned to the OSS for various secretarial and administrative duties. A remarkable recent coincidence led me to read the private memoir of one of these women, Rachel Johnson Bateson. She served first in Algiers and later in Caserta as assistant to Theodore Ryan, chief of SI Reports Section. She and one of her WAC friends became the favorites of Colonel Glavin and his executive officer, Norman Newhouse. The two officers and their companions traveled frequently to Capri and elsewhere, and their relationships must have been fairly well known in certain OSS circles, though not to me. What strikes me as amazing today is that after all these intervening years, another resident in the retirement community where my wife and I now live happened to tell me about this revealing memoir and loaned me her copy. It throws a light on another side of life in regimental headquarters of which I, in my youthful naiveté, had been oblivious.[25]

In the midst of the happiness following VE Day and the prospect of returning home, a tragedy befell one of the most popular and charming women on the Caserta staff, Susan Millett. While she and Kim Roosevelt were driving in the vicinity of Sorrento, his car overturned and Susan was killed. Her lively spirit and winning ways had captivated many of us fortunate enough to have known her, and we all felt a deep sense of loss. Although I was only one of her many admirers, I composed a poem that remained in my desk drawer until the writing of this memoir.

> Mimosa blooms along the way
> Along the way
> In early May
> And heavy sweet is all the air
> For there are orange blossoms fair
> And on the road below the hill
> The air is perfume-sweet and still.
>
> Palazzo San Leucio's crown
> Looks down and down
> Upon the town
> To where the plain is yellow-green
> And where the sea's blue-green between
> The mainland and the island queen
> The mountain-isle, the Leonine.
>
> From San Leucio to the sea
> The air is free
> Is warm and free
> But there is one too poor to pay
> To breathe that air for just one day
> Would I could pay the grave the fee
> That she might breathe the air with me.

Following VE Day on 8 May, the Caserta office began emptying out at a steadily increasing pace. Military personnel who had volunteered for service in the Far East were given priority transportation while other Caserta staffers were transferred to different OSS posts in Europe. I was not expecting priority air transport. But in early June during a visit to Caserta, General Donovan had told Colonel Glavin he was looking for candidates qualified to serve as his aide. A cable recommending me had been sent to Washington on 8 June. [26]

On 15 July, I received orders to report to OSS headquarters in Washington. Naturally, I was thrilled at the prospect of returning to family and friends, as well as the possibility of finally meeting General Donovan and serving as his aide. The general had acquired a reputation as a demanding and sometimes difficult taskmaster who thought nothing of calling his aide in the middle of the night with questions and long orders. The prestige of the aide's position went with a price tag of exhausting work, twenty-four hours a day. Everything would depend on the chemistry between Donovan and the candidate for aide.

Then, upon reporting into Washington headquarters, I learned that Donovan had already left for the Far East, and the aide search had been abandoned. The sense of letdown on hearing this news was soon overtaken by the promise of enjoying my home leave. If I had connected with the general and if he had chosen me as his aide, my life would have taken a different turn. Whether for better or for worse, I have never been able to resolve. What I do know for certain is that my time with the OSS in the Mediterranean was a golden moment for which I am forever thankful.

Epilogue

Sixty years of hindsight would seem to call for some comments about the significance of the events I witnessed in my tour of duty in the Mediterranean Theater. By chance I found myself in a position to observe developments that would influence the future of the intelligence community and U.S. interests in that part of the world, especially our relations with Italy.

The campaigns in the Mediterranean Theater of Operations were a proving ground, not only for the American military forces but also for the Office of Strategic Services. As a totally new endeavor for the United States, the OSS had to prove its worth to skeptics in both the military and political establishments of the era. Such skepticism still lingered in certain circles in Washington after the war, despite the organization's accomplishments. After the death of President Roosevelt, the skeptics had enough clout to obstruct his plans for a permanent intelligence organization.

On 20 September 1945, President Truman signed the order liquidating the OSS and dispersing its personnel to the Strategic Services Unit under the War Department, except for the Research and Analysis branch, which went to the State Department. Truman made what has often been called a tragic error because he misjudged the perilous international situation confronting postwar America and succumbed to critical views of the OSS both inside and outside the organization. One of the fiercest naysayers was J. Edgar Hoover, who despised Donovan and viewed the OSS as a threat to the Federal Bureau of Investigation. He was also convinced that Communists were scattered throughout the OSS.

Even before the end of the war, a charge tarnishing the OSS image and adding ammunition to Hoover's campaign against the organization began to surface, namely the Mafia connection. While Mussolini had been in power, the Mafia had been outlawed and aggressively pursued. After his overthrow in July 1943, however, the Mafia resumed operations in several of their former strongholds including Sicily, Naples, and Corsica. Controversy continues to this day over charges of Mafia connections among the many Italian-Americans serving in the OSS. The issue surfaced in 2004 in a French tome titled *The Corsican Godfathers* that details at great length the extent to which two Corsican families of cocaine dealers supported OSS activities in the south of France. The record of these associations—together with Donovan's willingness to admit his reliance on underworld recruitment, where necessary—raises awkward questions in discussions about how OSS experience can be applied to contemporary intelligence challenges.

In the fall of 1944, Hoover leaked to the arch-conservative *Chicago Tribune* a memorandum that Donovan had prepared at FDR's request outlining a plan for creation of a permanent intelligence service. The Chicago paper's subsequent attack on Roosevelt's concept led to a congressional uproar, prompting the president to table the matter. But one month before he died, FDR revived the idea and commissioned General Donovan to pull together all the government's intelligence elements and start mapping a plan for a permanent service. If he had lived, FDR would certainly have proceeded with something along the lines of the Donovan plan, and a more orderly transition of our intelligence assets would have been achieved.

Concerns about the aspirations of our wartime ally, the Soviet Union, began to intensify in the Truman administration as the war came to an end. Stopgap measures to restart a foreign intelligence function foundered in the State Department and the military establishment. Fortunately, however, the London office of OSS continued to function somewhat under the radar screen, primarily as a repository for the classified files generated during the war. On 24 January 1946, Truman established the Central Intelligence Group (CIG) under Rear Adm. Sidney Souers, but strictly as an intelligence collection agency without operational authority. The CIA was created a year and a half later by the National Security Act of July 1947, conforming in many respects to the concept outlined by Donovan in his December 1944 memorandum to President Roosevelt.

Thus began the transition from a temporary wartime agency, composed of amateurs, to a permanent one of professionals. Many of the former amateurs remained in the CIG and later the CIA, making their individual evolutions to professional status. I was one of those who chose to stay on through the succession of agencies leading to the CIA, where I served until 1949 before transferring into the Department of State.

Strangely enough, my transfer from the Agency to State took place because I happened to go to a Georgetown cocktail party. This switch illustrates the kind of easy maneuverability of personnel in the "good old days" just after the war. At this party, I met a fellow named Jack Kuhn who worked on a small staff in the office of the Secretary at State. Jack was in the process of transferring from this staff into the consular service. His boss, Jim Reber, had asked him to try to find a replacement for himself. Jack and I hit it off, and he said that I would be well qualified to fit into his slot. Even though I had an extremely interesting position in the CIA as analyst on the Russian desk, I had been thinking for some time that State would offer me a more promising career path than the Agency, mainly because of the opportunity to be part of the policymaking process. In short order, Kuhn set up an interview with Reber, and we also clicked. He asked me to join his staff, and in less than a month I was transferred into State where I served happily for the next five years.

Such an impromptu transfer as mine from one agency to another would be unimaginable in today's straitjacketed bureaucracy. It happened mainly because of my service in the OSS, where I had developed an interest in international affairs. Little did I realize while in Caserta that my work there, especially my involvement with the Italian partisans' activities, would be the first step on a course leading by stages into the office of the Secretary of State.

Through its operations in Italy, the OSS laid the groundwork for continuing friendship after the war between that country and the United States. The relationships with the Italian resistance that the large contingent of Italo-Americans established in Secret Intelligence, Special Operations, and Operational Groups were a major influence in strengthening those bonds. In Italy's turbulent postwar political evolution, a number of politicians whom the OSS had befriended came to power, keeping the country from siding with the Communists in the Cold War.

One of these politicians, Ferrucio Parri, who had played such a key role in Operation Sunrise, became the first prime minister after the war. He inherited an almost hopeless domestic situation. Having suffered enormous destruction from the longest campaign of the war, Italy was in shambles with few resources to start rebuilding until the Marshall Plan came into effect. Parri brought great energy and determination to his task, driving himself without letup—but he was not cut in the mold of a politician. Too rigid for compromise, he held scrupulously high moral standards, making his task difficult in the rough and tumble of Italian politics. He was eventually elected to a life term in the Italian senate, but even when his political path was in jeopardy, he acknowledged with gratitude the support that Italy had received from the United States during and after the war.

Clearly the Italian campaign has not received the credit it deserves as an essential element in the defeat of Nazi Germany. For example, the author of *The Sideshow War*, George Botjer, calls the outcome of the campaign a draw in which each side accomplished its main purposes. He argues that the Germans viewed their military objective in Italy as a delaying tactic, to tie up Allied forces and prevent them from encroaching on the boundaries of the Third Reich. And indeed it can be argued that until their surrender, the Germans accomplished that goal by keeping large Allied forces at bay and inflicting great losses on them.

The Allied campaign, according to Botjer's critique, was only a partial success. He faults it on two major grounds. Initially, the Allies mistakenly assumed that Italy would fall like a ripe plum, leading to a quick victory. Secondly, the campaign faltered because its objectives were never clearly defined. While the Allies were successful in tying down a dozen Wehrmacht divisions, the cost in lives and materiel was excessive, and the Allies never breached the Gothic Line until the German homeland was about to collapse. Most important, the Allies failed to launch a major attack from the south.

Certainly one of the main reasons for the failure to make more headway up the peninsula was the diversion of troops and materiel—American and British forces to the invasion of southern France and British forces to Greece, securing British interests there. The overriding fact remains, however, that for those Allied troops who fought and were lucky enough to survive in Italy, the final surrender seemed far more like a win than a draw. While there is certainly merit in the charge that the objectives were not clearly defined, clearly the Allies won and the Axis lost in Italy.

The importance of the Italian campaign and the entire Mediterranean Theater in winning World War II has been brilliantly presented in a long-overdue analysis appearing just as the writing of this memoir was nearing conclusion. In what *New York Times* book reviewer John Whiteclay Chambers II calls a major work of synthesis and interpretation (30 May 2004), military historian Douglas Porch has filled in an area neglected for more than six decades. This monumental work, *The Path to Victory: The Mediterranean Theater in World War II,* challenges all the commonly held beliefs that the campaigns of 1944–45 across northern Europe were virtually the only significant keys to winning the war. Covering the broad sweep of engagements in the Mediterranean from the 1942–43 assault on North Africa to all of the actions on the numerous islands and bordering states such as Greece and Yugoslavia, the book sheds a penetrating light on the Italian campaign. Porch makes the case that rather than being a sideshow, the Mediterranean Theater was a "pivotal theater for the Allies, one that made the difference between victory and defeat." The Porch book will serve as a vitally important means of correcting widespread misunderstanding of the relative importance of the major European campaign areas.

In the spring of 1965, twenty years after the 2 May surrender, Allen Dulles and a few others involved in Sunrise held a mini-reunion in Ascona, the very spot where the two Allied generals Lemnitzer and Airey met with Karl Wolff. The meeting provided an occasion to relive the events culminating in the surrender and to examine lessons learned from the experience. One of the principal points that Dulles made in his book *The Secret Surrender* is that even between nations at war, it is sometimes possible and even desirable that negotiations be conducted through secret channels between top-level representatives.

Sunrise did succeed in shortening the hostilities but only by a few days, not the longer period that Dulles originally envisioned. Because Roosevelt and

Churchill doubted the reliability of the German negotiators and feared alienating Stalin, they suspended the talks just when they might have been most productive. Had they been able to foresee Stalin's true colors after the war, they might well have been less deferential to him, and the Dulles scheme for ending the war might have come off sooner. The skills that Dulles displayed in finally bringing Sunrise to fulfillment marked him as an extraordinary mastermind of clandestine operations well qualified to serve as director of the CIA from 1953 to 1961.

The three main branches of the OSS that worked with partisan forces behind enemy lines were Secret Intelligence, Special Operations, and the Operational Groups. Their missions were intended to be complementary and mutually supporting. It was inevitable that as they evolved, an *esprit de corps* would develop within each branch and that rivalry between them would result. To the extent that rivalry promotes high standards of performance, it operates as a positive force. For the most part, this was the case with the three branches of the OSS. But misplaced or excessive competition can have a negative impact within an organization.

If there were negative effects resulting from inter-branch rivalry in OSS MEDTO, they were manifest less in the field than at top echelons. For example, SI Brindisi worked closely with the other two branches in arranging air operations for SO and OG teams as well as their own, and the teams worked in harmony behind the lines. In these high-risk environments, contention had to be avoided or kept to a minimum. However, senior officers at regimental or company headquarters levels were more likely to be competitive as they scrambled for the resources and influence to support their respective branches.

General Donovan's decision to establish three branches rather than the two of the British model (Secret Intelligence Service and Special Operations Executive) meant that there would be more duplication in command structure, communications, air support, personnel training, and so on. Despite such redundancy and the resulting rivalry, the three-branch approach produced impressive results in the Mediterranean Theater.

As the writing of this book was winding down in the spring of 2004, the nation was facing increasingly grave challenges in the war on terrorism. The role of intelligence and the myriad intelligence agencies supporting that war were receiving intense scrutiny and criticism from many quarters. The United States was being criticized for a range of serious intelligence failures—those leading up to the war as well as those associated with the conduct of it.

In comparison with later wars, World War II has come to be regarded as "the good war"—a more conventional conflict with enemies who, however deadly and threatening, were identifiable and eventually containable. Today the military might of the United States, by far the most powerful and richest nation on earth, is proving less and less of an advantage in the global ideological conflict. In the words of World War II–era comic strip character Pogo, "We have met the enemy and he is us." U.S. power and influence are the very objects of spreading animosity toward America and its values.

The techniques and systems that the OSS developed during World War II proved a valuable asset in winning that war, and they were passed on to successor agencies in the intelligence community. The CIA, in particular, acknowledges the direct heritage of its predecessor, the OSS. In the intervening years, the intelligence community has grown into a vast bureaucratic complex of distinct and often competing agencies whose very size and tangled relationships impede their effective pursuit of mission. The bipartisan 9/11 Commission and many knowledgeable observers have called our intelligence community broken and bloated. The rocky start of hastily enacting the major organizational changes proposed by the commission in the fall of 2004 did not bode well for the prospect of constructive reform.

In discussing these organizational problems, a question is often asked how the lessons learned by the OSS in World War II can be applied today. Unfortunately, such discussions often fail to recognize the vast sea change that has altered the U.S. geopolitical status in recent decades. As a fledgling organization operating with relatively few restraints and improvising its own methods and procedures, wherever and whenever needed, the OSS ran its own show to a remarkable degree. Moreover, Donovan was not known as Wild Bill without cause. He relied heavily on his close personal connection with FDR to achieve his goals. The OSS scored a good number of successes, but many operations failed, sometimes with disastrous results.

The postwar era also witnessed increased congressional interest in overseeing the OSS's successors in the intelligence community. Whatever the OSS may have enjoyed in the way of a free hand during World War II came to be sharply curtailed, for better or for worse. For example, a complicated system evolved governing the release of presidential covert "lethal findings" that authorized the removal of designated individuals. In World War II, few such constraints existed. As the checks and balances of our threefold democratic system have been reinforced, the government's capacity to carry out the intelligence function and to wage war has been dramatically altered from that of World War II. We cannot turn back the clock to the time of "the good war," and a looming question arises as to whether time is our ally in the ideological conflict now confronting us.

Appendix: Chronology

Political and Military Milestones

13 June 1942, President Roosevelt establishes the Office of Strategic Services by executive order

22 October 1942, Gen. Mark Clark is landed on beach near Algiers

November 1942, Operation Torch, the Allied invasion of North Africa

4 November 1942, Rommel's retreat from El Alamein

14 January 1943, Casablanca Conference

9 July 1943, Allied invasion of Sicily

14 July 1943, Bastille Day, maquis proclaim the Free Republic of Vercors

24 July 1943, overthrow of Mussolini, who is succeeded by Marshall Badoglio

3 September 1943, U.S.-Italian armistice signed

9 September 1943, Allied invasion of Salerno

12 September 1943, German parachutists rescue Mussolini

November 1943, Tehran Conference

December 1943, Cairo Conference, Combined Chiefs of Staff commit to Operation Overlord

4 June 1944, fall of Rome

16 June 1944, Ivanoe Bonomi assumes office of premier of Italy

My Assignments

13 May 1943, I graduate from Fort Sill officer candidate school

November 1943, OSS recruits me from Field Artillery Regimental Training Center, Fort Bragg

November 1943 to April 1944, train in five OSS camps around Washington

1 April 1944, sail from Newport News bound for Suez

Political and Military Milestones

and announces formation of a new CLN government

11 August 1944, Germans evacuate Florence

16 August 1944, Operation Dragoon invasion of southern France

mid-November 1944, Gen. Harold Alexander calls for stand-down of partisan activity in northern Italy

20 November 1944, three delegates of CLNAI travel to Caserta to negotiate agreement with AFHQ on support of their coalition

December 1944, six Italian political parties consolidate in the CLNAI as an extension of the Bonomi government in northern Italy

1 January 1945, Germans capture Ferrucio Parri, hiding undercover in Milan

19 February 1945, OSS Secret Intelligence branch moves its base from Brindisi to Siena

8 March 1945, Germans release Parri to initiate surrender negotiations with Allen Dulles

10 April 1945, Allies launch spring offensive in northern Italy

12 April 1945, President Roosevelt dies

5 May 1945, German surrender, VE Day

My Assignments

14–27 May 1944, OSS Cairo

27 May–21 September 1944, OSS Algiers

21 September 1944, transferred from OSS Algiers to OSS Caserta

28 September–3 October 1944, serve as escort officer for Papaya mission to Annecy, France, then on to Paris, and back via Lyon to Caserta

11 October 1944, assigned mission to OSS Siena

28 October 1944, R and R, OSS Capri

27 November 1944, assigned mission to OSS Bari and Brindisi

8 February 1945, assigned mission to OSS Florence

17 February 1945, travel orders to OSS Switzerland (travel canceled)

23 February 1945, travel orders to Annemasse and Paris

4 March 1945, travel orders to proceed to Caserta (from where not indicated)

5 May 1945, assigned mission to Florence

20 June 1945, assigned mission to Venice and "such other places in Italy as may be necessary"

15 July 1945, travel orders to Washington

Notes

Chapter 1

1. John Birn was transferred to the Far East. Serving with distinction, he was promoted to first lieutenant and awarded the Thailand Commendation. After the ceasefire, Birn took the Thai military surrender in the Royal Palace in Bangkok.
2. Norman Randolph Turpin went to Italy, where he parachuted behind enemy lines to conduct a highly successful mission, after which a British submarine exfiltrated him and his teammates. He then volunteered for Infantry combat duty in the Far East and was sent to the Philippines. Turpin was killed there, just before the end of the war, while leading his men against a group of Japanese snipers.
3. "Job Record," report by William Underwood, 7 January 1944, NARA Ref. Entry 092A, Box 00105, Folder 02220, Shelf 190: 38/18/02.

Chapter 2

1. Kermit Roosevelt, *War Report of the OSS,* vol. 2, *The Overseas Targets* (New York: Walker, 1976), 47–50.
2. Artemis Cooper, *Cairo in the War, 1939–1945* (London: Hamish Hamilton, 1989), 223–26.
3. Letter to the author from Jill Stix, widow of Tom, confirming the facts of his mission to Greece, 19 April 2002.

Chapter 3

1. Joseph E. Persico, *Roosevelt's Secret War: FDR and World War II Espionage* (New York: Random House, 2001), 214–15.
2. R. Harris Smith, *OSS: The Secret History of America's First Central Intelligence Agency* (Berkeley and Los Angeles: University of California Press, 1972), 51.
3. Smith, *OSS,* 180.
4. Albert R. Materazzi, "OSS Operational Groups in Italy, 1943–1945," preface to a draft paper written by a member of Operational Group A. OSS web site, 15 Sept. 2004. http://www.osssociety.org/
5. Max Corvo, *The OSS in Italy, 1942–1945: A Personal Memoir* (New York: Praeger, 1990), 115. For another account of the Operational Groups in Algiers, see Roosevelt's *War Report of the OSS,* vol. 2, 170.
6. See also Smith, *OSS,* 179–80.
7. Tentative functional chart of American officers at SPOC, NARA Ref. RG 226, E 190, Folder 761.

8. Ian Sutherland, "The OSS Operational Groups: Origin of Army Special Forces," *Special Warfare* (the professional bulletin of the John F. Kennedy Special Warfare Center and School, June 2002). This article is an incisive portrayal of the organization and operations of the French Operational Groups, as well as being a testimony to the concept of OGs as the antecedents of today's Special Forces.

9. By the time Underwood and Rutherford were dropped to their target area just above the Pyrenees, the area had been almost completely liberated. The only radio signal ever received from them said, "Wonderful drop. Cornfield." We learned later that with no Germans around, they spent most of their time being fêted by the partisans, who plied them with foie gras and champagne.

10. Smith, *OSS,* 186–88.

11. Winston S. Churchill, *Triumph and Tragedy* (Boston: Houghton Mifflin, 1959), 62–64.

12. Ibid., 68.

13. History of Alice Team, prepared for report "OSS Aid to the French Resistance in World War II," Operational Group Command, Company B, 671st Special Reconnaissance Battalion, Separate (Provisional), Grenoble, France, 20 September 1944, 20.

14. Maj. John W. Shaver III, "Office of Strategic Services, Operational Groups in France during World War II, July–October 1944" (master's thesis presented to U.S. Army Command and General Staff College, Fort Leavenworth, Kansas, 1993), 1.

15. "OSS Aid to the French Resistance in World War II," Report on Operational Groups, Company B-2671st Special Reconnaissance Battalion, Grenoble, France, 20 September 1944, 10.

16. Mercenary Mission File at National Archives, NARA Ref. OSS OP 0058 190, Box 00128, Folder 00685, Shelf 190.

17. Final report of the SPOC Debriefing Operation, signed by Lt. Col. Kenneth Baker, 15 November 1944, NARA Ref. RG 226, Entry 190, Box 135, Folder 767.

18. Corvo, *The OSS in Italy,* 71.

19. "Reorganization of OSS Activities in the Mediterranean Theater," internal memorandum of 2677th Regiment headquarters, 16 August 1944, to Col. John E. Toulmin (unsigned).

Chapter 4

1. George Botjer, *Sideshow War: The Italian Campaign, 1943–1945* (College Station: Texas A & M University Press, 1996), 22–23.

2. Churchill, *Triumph and Tragedy,* 65.

3. George C. Chalou, *The Secrets War: The Office of Strategic Services in WWII* (Washington, D.C.: National Archives and Records Administration, 1992),

183–94. This book also includes an article entitled "Are Human Spies Superfluous?" by Peter Tompkins (129–39), an OSS agent fluent in Italian who entered Rome well before the Allied assault. He directed activities of partisan groups and provided intelligence to all the Allied forces convening on the city.

4. Churchill, *Triumph and Tragedy*, 727–28. See also *Closing of the Ring* by Churchill (Boston: Houghton Mifflin, 1951), 116–17.

5. Botjer, *Sideshow War*, 60–65.

6. Ibid., 151.

7. Orders issued by Company A (Rear Echelon), 2677th Regiment, Office of Strategic Services (Provisional), U.S. Army, 21 September 1944.

8. Orders issued by Headquarters Allied Armies in Italy (U.S. Contingent), Ovhd, 27 September 1944.

9. Report on mission of 1st Lt. E. H. Kloman Jr. to France, 28 September 1944 to 3 October 1944, Headquarters 2677th Regiment OSS (Provisional), Kloman files. While this book was nearing completion, a friend of mine, Tia Sidey, provided information on Captain Mathieu, who was the father of her stepbrother. Born in Sardinia, Arturo Carlo Felice Mathieu II came from a family that had left France during the Napoleonic era. He was known to be trilingual, speaking French, Italian, and English. He became an American citizen and was studying for a Ph.D. at Princeton before he enlisted in the Army. His OSS personnel file was probably lost in the 1973 fire that burned these records in St. Louis, Missouri. Thus, Mrs. Sidey has been unable to ascertain details on Captain Mathieu's OSS service or how he died. There are two conflicting accounts of his death: one that he was killed in an accident when his Jeep ran off the road into a stream, and the other that he was shot in neutral Switzerland while on assignment. A surviving record of his possessions at the time of death indicates that he was carrying substantial amounts in several currencies.

10. Corvo, *The OSS in Italy*, 206–9.

11. Roosevelt, *War Report of the OSS*, 231–33.

12. Report on Kloman mission.

13. Theater officer pouch review, 24 September 1944, McGivern to Hoffman, NARA.

14. Smith, *OSS*, 103.

15. Ibid.

16. Studs Terkel, *The Good War: An Oral History of World War II* (New York: Pantheon Books, 1971), 495.

17. Travel orders, 2677th Regiment, 11 October 1944, to 1st Lt. Erasmus H. Klowman *(sic)*.

18. Patrick K. O'Donnell, *OSS: The Unknown Story of the Men and Women of WWII's OSS* (New York: Free Press, 2004), 132.

19. Botjer, *Sideshow War*, 131.

20. Corvo, *The OSS in Italy,* 177.
21. Ibid., 192.
22. Botjer, *Sideshow War,* 51.
23. Roosevelt, *War Report of the OSS,* 195.
24. Robert W. Winks, *Cloak and Gown: Scholars in the Secret War, 1939–1961* (New York: William Morrow, 1987), 187.
25. Ibid., 167.
26. History of the Operations Section 2677th Regiment OSS (Provisional) in Italy, NARA Ref. 154, Box 56, Folder 941.
27. Memorandum from Maj. Walter M. Ross, commanding officer Company B, to chief, Operations, 2677th Regiment, 30 November 1944, Kloman files.
28. Cable 145 from Rome to Caserta, 20 November 1944, Ref. RG 226, Entry 210, Box 134, F.4.
29. Cable 184 Glavin from Newhouse, 25 November 1944, NARA Ref. RG 226, Entry 210, Box 134, F.4.
30. Botjer, *Sideshow War,* 152.
31. Letter from Maj. William G. Suhling Jr. to commanding officer 2677th Regiment. Subject: Communist agents, 10 November 1944.
32. Corvo, *The OSS in Italy,* 269.
33. Ibid., 218.

Chapter 5

1. Internal 2677th Regiment memorandum from Maj. Norman Newhouse to Operations and six other offices. Subject: CLNAI, dated 17 January 1945, NARA Ref. RG 226, Entry 210, Box 134, F.4.
2. Annemasse cable 152, Baker to Glavin and Kloman, NARA Ref. RG 226, Entry 210, Box 134, F.4.
3. Smith, *OSS,* 109.
4. Travel orders, 2677th Regiment, 8 February 1945, Kloman files.
5. Memorandum, AFHQ 2677th Regiment, Field Base F, 29 March 1945, Gen. Mark Clark's call to arms, NARA Ref. RG 226, Entry 210, Box 134, F.4.
6. Recommendation for Award, To the War Department, A.G.O. Washington 25 DC, 13; September 1945 Cables 1221, 22 February; and 930, 23 February, Wood in Caserta to Suhling in Florence, NARA.
7. Corvo, *The OSS in Italy,* 197–98.
8. "Dropping Zones in Northern Italy," memorandum from Maj. Judson B. Smith, operations officer, Company D, 2677th Regiment, to Lt. E. H. Kloman, 20 March 1945, NARA Ref. RG 226, Entry 190, Box 131.
9. "Air Operations Review, March 1944–April 1945," report to Maj. Judson

B. Smith from Lt. B. M. Cave, USNR, Air Operations Officer, NARA Ref. RG 226, Entry 154, Box 56, Folder 941.

10. "Minutes of March 7 meeting with Mr. Dugoni," memorandum from Maj. Judson Smith, Operations Officer, Company D, to 2677th Regiment, 9 March 1945, NARA.

11. Chalou, *The Secrets War,* 192.

12. Allen Dulles, *The Secret Surrender* (New York: Harper and Row, 1966), 239–47.

13. Lynn H. Nicholas, *The Rape of Europa: The Fate of Europe's Treasures in the Third Reich and the Second World War* (New York: Knopf, 1994), 257, 268–70.

14. Churchill, *Triumph and Tragedy,* 441.

15. Corvo, *The OSS in Italy,* 255–56.

16. Dulles, *The Secret Surrender,* 244–45.

17. Corvo, *The OSS in Italy,* 270.

18. Travel orders for Florence, 2677th Regiment, 5 May 1945, to 1st Lt. Erasmus H. Kloman, Kloman files.

19. Cable from Comzone France to AFHQ, for director OSS, recommending travel for 1st Lt. Erasmus H. Kloman to Berne, 17 February 1945, Kloman files.

20. My search of the archives did lead me to another document, a history of the Operations Section of Company D that presents an objective view of OSS Italian operations from a vantage point closer to the front lines than regimental headquarters in Caserta. It is unsigned, undated, and unclassified. NARA Ref. 154, Box 56, Folder 941.

21. Memorandum to secretariat 2677th Regiment, OSS, signed by Maj. Judson B. Smith, chief Special Operations, and Capt. E. H. Kloman Jr., acting Operations officer, 15 July 1945, NARA.

22. Corvo, *The OSS in Italy,* 277. The introduction to Corvo's book contains a detailed critique of the many histories of OSS and its founder, General Donovan. It lays out the reasons for which, after 1982, Corvo decided to write his own history in a book that was eight years in the making.

23. Smith, *OSS,* 121–22.

24. Headquarters 2677th Regiment, by order of Colonel Glavin, 20 June 1945, Kloman files.

25. Rachel Johnson Bateson, "Vignettes and Lagniappe," private memoir, 1984, Kloman files.

26. Cable 5197, Newhouse for Glavin to 109 (code designation for Donovan), 8 June 1945: "Captain Kloman, Acting Operations Officer here since March will be available shortly. Glavin recommends him as an intelligent, capable, industrious staff officer and believes he will be most satisfactory."

Bibliography

Alsop, Stewart, and Thomas Braden. *Sub Rosa: The OSS and American Espionage.* New York: Reynal and Hitchcock, 1946.

Botjer, George. *Sideshow War: The Italian Campaign, 1943–1945.* College Station: Texas A & M University Press, 1996.

Brown, Anthony Cave. *Bodyguard of Lies.* New York: Harper and Row, 1975.

Chalou, George C. *The Secrets War: The Office of Strategic Services in WWII.* Washington, D.C.: National Archives and Records Administration, 1992.

Churchill, Winston S. *Closing of the Ring.* Boston: Houghton Mifflin, 1951.

———. *Triumph and Tragedy.* Boston: Houghton Mifflin, 1959.

Cline, Ray S. *Secrets, Spies, and Scholars: Blueprint of the Essential CIA.* Washington, D.C.: Acropolis Books, 1976.

Cooper, Artemis. *Cairo in the War, 1939–1945.* London: Hamish Hamilton, 1989.

Corvo, Max. *The OSS in Italy, 1942–1945: A Personal Memoir.* New York: Praeger, 1990.

Dulles, Allen. *The Craft of Intelligence.* New York: Harper and Row, 1963.

———. *The Secret Surrender.* New York: Harper and Row, 1966.

Hall, Roger. *You're Stepping on My Cloak and Dagger.* New York: W. W. Norton, 1957.

Hitz, Frederick P. *The Great Game: The Myth and the Reality of Espionage.* New York: Knopf, 2004.

Ireland, Bernard. *War in the Mediterranean, 1940–1943.* Annapolis, Md.: Naval Institute Press, 2004.

Keegan, John. *Intelligence in War: Knowledge of the Enemy, from Napoleon to Al Qaeda.* New York: Knopf, 2003.

Kehoe, Robert R. "An Allied Team with the French Resistance in 1944." *Studies in Intelligence.* Journal of the American Intelligence Community, Washington, D.C., Special Sixtieth Anniversary Edition, Office of Strategic Services, 2000.

Kesselring, Albert. *Memoirs of Marshall Kesselring.* Novato, Calif.: Presidio Press, 1989.

Larrabee, Eric. *Commander in Chief: Franklin Delano Roosevelt, His Lieutenants, and Their War.* Annapolis, Md.: Naval Institute Press, 2004.

Lindsay, Franklin. *Beacons in the Night: With the OSS and Tito's Partisans in Wartime Yugoslavia.* Stanford: Stanford University Press, 1983.

Macksey, Kenneth. *Kesselring: German Master Strategist of the Second World War.* London: Greenhill Books, 2000.

Materazzi, Albert R. "OSS Operational Groups in Italy, 1943–1945." Preface to a draft paper written by a member of Operational Group A. OSS web site, 15 Sept. 2004. http://www.osssociety.org/

McIntosh, Elizabeth P. *Sisterhood of Spies: The Women of the OSS.* Annapolis, Md.: Naval Institute Press, 1998.

Meacham, Jon. *Franklin and Winston: An Intimate Portrait of an Epic Friendship.* New York: Random House, 2003.

Nicholas, Lynn H. *The Rape of Europa: The Fate of Europe's Treasures in the Third Reich and the Second World War.* New York: Knopf, 1994.

O'Donnell, Patrick K. *OSS: The Unknown Story of the Men and Women of WWII's OSS.* New York: Free Press, 2004.

O'Toole, G. J. A. *Honorable Treachery: A History of U.S. Intelligence, Espionage, and Covert Action, from the American Revolution to the CIA.* New York: Atlantic Monthly Press, 1991.

Persico, Joseph E. *Roosevelt's Secret War: FDR and World War II Espionage.* New York: Random House, 2001.

Pinck, Daniel C., Geoffrey M. T. Jones, and Charles T. Pinck, eds. *Stalking the History of the Office of Strategic Services: An OSS Bibliography.* Boston: OSS/Donovan Press, 2000.

Porch, Douglas. *The Path to Victory: The Mediterranean Theater in World War II.* New York: Farrar Strauss Giroux, 2004.

Roosevelt, Kermit. *War Report of the OSS.* Vol. 2, *The Overseas Targets.* New York: Walker, 1976.

Shaver, Maj. John W. III. "Office of Strategic Services, Operational Groups in France during World War II, July–October 1944." Master's thesis presented to U.S. Army Command and General Staff College, Fort Leavenworth, Kans., 1993.

Singlaub, John. *Hazardous Duty: An American Soldier in the Twentieth Century.* New York: Summit, 1991.

Smith, R. Harris. *OSS: The Secret History of America's First Central Intelligence Agency.* Berkeley and Los Angeles: University of California Press, 1972.

Stevenson, William. *A Man Called Intrepid: The Incredible WWII Narrative of the Hero Whose Spy Network and Diplomacy Changed the Course of History.* New York: Lyons Press, 1976.

Sutherland, Ian. "The OSS Operational Groups: Origin of Army Special Forces." *Special Warfare.* The professional bulletin of the John F. Kennedy Special Warfare Center and School, June 2002.

Terkel, Studs. *The Good War: An Oral History of World War II.* New York: Pantheon Books, 1971.

"Trip to General Wolff's HQ, 9–12 May 1945." Report of T. S. Ryan, special liaison officer, to commanding officer 2677th Regiment OSS (Provisional), APO 512 U.S Army, 1 June 1945. Four attachments. Declassified 8/2/56.

Troy, Thomas. *Donovan and the CIA: A History of the Establishment of the Central Intelligence Agency.* Foreign Intelligence Book Series. Frederick, Md.: University Publications of America, 1981.

Waller, John H. *The Unseen War in Europe: Espionage and Conspiracy in the Second World War.* New York: Random House, 1996.

Winks, Robert W. *Cloak and Gown: Scholars in the Secret War, 1939–1961.* New York: William Morrow, 1987.

Index

Note: Italicized page numbers indicate illustrations, tables, or photos. Page numbers followed by the letter *n,* plus a number, refer to endnotes.

AAI (Allied Armies in Italy), 50
Action Party, 66, 75, 79
AFHQ. *See* Allied Forces Headquarters
Airey, Terence, 86, 87, 105
Air Operations Section: British, 66–67; OSS, 31, 83
Air Resupply Detachment (ARSD), 50, 71
air transportation, competition for, 66–67, 71, 106
Alexander, Harold, 39, 40, 52, 74–75, 90
Algeria, liberation of, 26–28
Algiers: daily life in, 26, 36, 50–51; OSS operations in, 17, 24, 28–31, *29;* U.S. intelligence forces in, 26. *See also* Special Projects Operations Center (SPOC), Algiers
Alice operational group, 40–46, *41, 45*
Allied Armies in Italy (AAI), 50
Allied Control Commission, 71
Allied Forces Headquarters (AFHQ): in Caserta, 49–50, 73; in North Africa, 28, 30, 33–34; reputation of SI in, 64–65
Annemasse, 61, 79, 81, 82
Anzio, Allied landing at, 56
Area B, 10
Area F, 6–7, *9, 29*
ARSD (Air Resupply Detachment), 50, 71
art treasures, Italian, 80–81, 86, 92
Audisio, Walter, 90
Avignon, debriefing at, 48–49

Badoglio, Pietro, 30, 54, 55, 56, 57, 64, 71
Baker, Kenneth, 34–35, 49, 61, 79
Birn, John, 4, 7, 111n1 (chap. 1)
bombing: by Allies, 43–44, 84; by Germans, 15, *1*
Bonomi, Ivanoe, 57, 72
Botjer, George, 57, 104–5
Brennan, Earl, 53
Brindisi, 50, 55, 64, 65, 66, 67, 71, 106

British forces, in Egypt, 16, 20–21
British intelligence forces: branches of, 14; coordination with Allies, 24, 38–39; in Egypt, 16; as experienced veterans, xii, 7, 21; German surrender and, 85; rivalry with U.S. forces, 66–67, 71, 72; socialist partisans and, 72, 73; training assistance from, 6–7
Bruce, David, 53

Cadorna, Raffaele, 57–58, 73, 81
Cairo, Egypt: Allied forces in, 16–17, 20, *20;* daily life in, 20–24, *22;* OSS activities in, 17–20, 24–25; OSS training in, 17–19, *19*
Capri, 67–70, 95
Carnegie–U.S. Steel, 11
Casablanca: Allied summit in, 27, 52; U.S. intelligence forces in, 26
Caserta: Allied Forces Headquarters move to, 49–50; architecture and art of, 58–59, *59;* closing of station at, 95; daily life in, 63, *77,* 77–78; German surrender at, 90–91; OSS activities, 59–62, 65–67, 70–71, 73, 79, 80–81, 82, 94–96; OSS facilities, 58–59; OSS move to, 49–50; OSS organization and staff, 62–65
Caserta Agreement, 73
Central Intelligence Agency (CIA), 103, 106, 107
Central Intelligence Group (CIG), 103
Churchill, Winston: in Casablanca, 27; on Italy invasion, 52, 53, 56, 66; on North Africa invasion, 27; and Operation Sunrise, 88, 93, 105–6; policies on monarchies, 73; and postwar zones of influence, 74; on SOE, 14; and southern France invasion, 39, 40
CIA (Central Intelligence Agency), 103, 106, 107

121

About the Author

Erasmus Kloman received a B.A. from Princeton, an M.A. from Harvard, and a Ph.D. from the University of Pennsylvania. His professional career engaged him in government, academia, and private business. After his wartime experience in the Office of Strategic Services and postwar experience in its successor, the Central Intelligence Agency, he spent five years in the Department of State, followed by five years in the Foreign Policy Research Institute at the University of Pennsylvania. From there he moved into the international business world, where he worked as a corporate executive for three firms, AMAX, IBM, and the Diebold Group. In each of these firms he served in the senior corporate offices as a public affairs officer and writer. In 1969 he returned to Washington to serve as a Senior Research Associate in the National Academy of Public Administration. In his twenty years since retirement he has pursued a dual career as a painter and writer. His art has been exhibited in various venues from Washington to New England. He has written three travel books about France, which are augmented by his own artwork.